MEL BROOKS
AND THE
SPOOF MOVIE

NICK SMURTHWAITE
& PAUL GELDER

PROTEUS BOOKS
London and New York

PROTEUS BOOKS is an imprint of
The Proteus Publishing Group

United States
PROTEUS PUBLISHING CO., INC.
9 West 5th Street, Suite 4504
New York, NY 10019

distributed by:
THE SCRIBNER BOOK COMPANIES, INC.
597 Fifth Avenue
New York, NY 10017

United Kingdom
PROTEUS (PUBLISHING) LIMITED
Bremar House,
Sale Place
London W2 1PT

ISBN 0 86276 049 6 (paperback)
      0 86276 050 X (hardback)

First published in U.S. 1982
First published in U.K. 1982

Design **Sharmans**
Typeset **SX Composing Ltd**
Printed **by Printer Industria Grafica sa, Barcelona, Spain**
D.L.B. 29276–1982

CONTENTS

INTRODUCTION

Alfred Hitchcock defined drama as life with all the dull bits left out. Spoof, you might say, is life with the dull bits left out and the dramatic bits sent up. It makes no claims to significance, no pleas for serious consideration. And yet it has emerged, in the last two decades, as a quite distinct and legitimate cinematic form, as manifest as road movies or shlock horror.

Reputable directors like Roman Polanski, Joseph Losey, John Huston, Alan Parker and Steven Spielberg have been attracted to the spoof, with its appealing blend of affection and irreverence. Why? Perhaps they find it an escape from the introspection of serious film-making, a sort of celluloid therapy. The spoof enables a director to poke fun at the conventions and conceits of Hollywood, to bite the hand that feeds him. It can even be a form of revenge, an effective (and profitable) way of expressing the ambivalence, anger and frustration a director feels towards the whole business. More often, though, it is a way of showing admiration and gratitude for a durable genre (western, horror, thriller) or one particular director of distinction (De Mille, Hitchcock, Bergman).

No popular art form is so vulnerable to self parody as the cinema. That incongruous blend of high finance, low taste and artistic aspiration offers an open invitation to ridicule and scorn. As Ethel Barrymore said, when she first arrived in Hollywood in the early thirties: 'The people are unreal, the flowers are unreal, the fruit is unreal . . . the whole place is a glaring, gaudy nightmarish set, built up in the middle of the desert.' No wonder so many stars have come to grief, unable to cope with the pressures of constantly living a lie. The big studios create their own demi-gods, worshipped by the faceless legion of fans. Only a handful of stars have managed to avoid the fatal trap of believing their own publicity. The others, like Joan Crawford and Errol Flynn, became grotesque caricatures of the images they projected on the screen.

There have been many realistic satires of the movie world – *Sunset Boulevard*, *The Big Knife*, *Inside Daisy Clover*, *All About Eve*, *S.O.B.* to name a few – but in this book we shall be dealing with the genre spoofs, the Mel Brooks School of Spoof, which is dedicated to the notion that no movie myth is too sacred to be spared a little

parody – or in Mel Brooks's case, a lot of parody.

The problem, of course, is deciding what constitutes a spoof since there are many films that contain elements of parody without actually falling into that category. The Bond films are a case in point. No doubt Ian Fleming intended his novels to suspend disbelief, but the intrepid 007 has developed, on the screen, into a two-dimensional strip cartoon character whose cool indestructibility is second only to Superman. The stunts have become more and more extravagant, the subsidiary characters increasingly bizarre. What keeps it from being 'pure' spoof is that the plot still takes precedence over the jokes, but only just. The same was true of Dick Lester's Musketeer films, where the director's irrepressible sense of fun, and his reluctance to take anything seriously was in danger of stemming the narrative flow. Of course that's nothing new in the movies.

Some critics argue that Hitchcock has been his own best parodist for years, certainly in his later films, *Frenzy* and *Family Plot* (the car careering downhill, brakes kaput, was worthy of Mel Brooks) and a spoof of almost any Ken Russell movie could hardly be more far-fetched than the originals; think of Glenda Jackson's carpet clawing scene in *The Music Lovers* and every other scene in *The Devils*.

Indeed cinema history is littered with spoofs which turned out to be half as funny as the films that inspired them, recent examples being *The Last Re-Make of Beau Jeste* (1977), *Zorro the Gay Blade* (1980) and *Airplane!*(1979). How can you hope to parody a film as sublimely silly as *Airport '75*? Presumably the studio which made *Airplane!* realising that no-one took the Airport movies seriously any more (if they ever did) decided to go for bust with a full-blown spoof.

In the early days, movie spoofs were used as vehicles for the likes of Laurel and Hardy, the Marx Brothers, and W. C. Fields, artistes who were more popular and familiar to audiences than the various cinematic genres. They were gentle, innocuous send-ups like *Sons of the Desert* (1939), *Go West* (1940) and *My Little Chickadee* (1940), with no other purpose than providing a recognisable scenario in which to be funny. The mordant wit of Fields and Groucho Marx gave their films an edge, but they cut little

ice as parodies.

The 'vehicle' tradition continued into the forties with Abbott and Costello, masters of Vaudevillian cross-talk and funny business, the natural successors to Laurel and Hardy, though not it would seem heirs to that partnership's lasting universal popularity. At the time, however, their *Abbott and Costello Meets . . .* series was water-tight box office, rivalled only by the Hope and Crosby partnership, a winning blend of spoof, shmaltz and slapstick, memorable more for the couple's jibes at each other than any attempt to aim for larger targets. In later chapters we shall be discussing how these exclusively male comedy teams – some obviously heterosexual, some open to speculation – influenced and inspired Mel Brooks, most of whose style derives from the Vaudevillian tradition of Laurel and Hardy, and the Marx Brothers.

Not until the sixties was it generally accepted that the American cinema is made up of genres and, ironically, it was that acceptance which spawned the spoof genre, because many film directors had become too self-conscious to take themselves and their European peers seriously. This is especially true of the crime thriller genre, which sparked off an enormous number of spoofs, from John Huston's excellent *Beat the Devil* (1954), starring Humphrey Bogart, right through to the Pink Panther series, which found such a loyal following that it became almost a genre of its own devising. Peter Sellers finished up spoofing his own creation.

With some notable exceptions – *Love and Death* (1975), *Bugsy Malone* (1976), *Movie Movie* (1979) – it is the horror genre that has inspired the best spoofs. One thinks of Polanski's *Dance of the Vampires* (1969), in which the lovely Sharon Tate made her last screen appearance; *The Rocky Horror Picture Show* (1975), a cult success on both sides of the Atlantic; *Love at First Bite* (1979), with George Hamilton as the suavest Count Dracula ever to draw blood; and *An American Werewolf in London* (1981), an extraordinary mix of tongue-in-cheek humour and genuine horror flick effects, which somehow contrived to work.

The success of this last film, both commercially and artistically, may provide the key to the appeal of spoof. It managed to satisfy

*George Hamilton as the super-smooth vampire aristocrat in
Love at First Bite.*

the twin appetites of today's consumer for both illusion and reality. In other words, as we watched the totally realistic transformation of David Naughton from a wholesome all-American boy into a slavering werewolf, which once would have been accepted at face value, we were simultaneously aware of the absurdity of such a process. We have become the victims of our own sophistication. Directors can no longer rely on the gullibility and innocence which made movie-going such an unqualified pleasure in the early days. Since the war audiences have become progressively more worldly and detached, making it more and more difficult for film-makers to suspend our disbelief. We have become a race of sceptics, distrustful of politicians' promises and eager to see them discredited and lampooned.

In England the era of disillusionment was ushered in by the university satirists – Peter Cook, Dudley Moore, David Frost, Jonathan Miller and co. – whose comic anarchy ran the gauntlet of a startled English establishment. The effect was a rapid loss of political dignity and credibility, backed up (and prolonged) by the emergence of a fearless satirical magazine, Private Eye, which specialises in toppling the high and mighty, whether they deserve it or not.

In the States the ascendancy of an ageing, second-rate Hollywood actor to the highest political office in the land has done little to reaffirm public confidence in the Presidency. There are many parallels to be drawn between politics and showbiz, but even the most committed actor in England would be laughed out of circulation for aspiring to the Prime Ministership.

It is this reluctance to take anything seriously that has made the spoof such a popular form. And yet the success of a TV series like *Dallas* on the one hand and *Soap* on the other, probably appealing to the same mass audience, shows that we have become more than a little schizo-phrenic in our susceptibilities, wanting the 'real' distortion of life in *Dallas* one minute, and the spoof distortion of *Soap* the next. That other durable series, *M.A.S.H.*, manages the same feat as *An American Werewolf in London*, dealing with serious matters in a frivolous way.

Advertising and hype has exerted a good deal

Will he or won't he . . . Frankenstein invites the elements to activate his monster.

of influence here, always quick to exploit a mood or trend, whatever the moral implications. Many reputable film directors started out directing commercials – Richard Lester, Alan Parker, Hugh Hudson – and their work in this field is as impressive in its own way as anything on the big screen. Sophisticates may pretend to be unaffected by advertising, but even the most resilient of us is prey to the relentless onslaught of the ad-men. The critic Pauline Kael blames advertising for the decline of popular film-making, comparing the slick unreality of many contemporary movies to 'the commercials no-one believes'. In her 1965 essay 'Against Spoofing', Miss Kael wrote that the vogue for parody derived from a loss of confidence on the director's part that anybody would accept serious intent any longer:

> 'Spoofing has become the safety net for those who are unsure of their footing. Unlike satire, spoofing has no serious objectives: it doesn't attack anything that anyone could take seriously; it has no cleansing power. It's just a technique of ingratiation: the spoof apologizes for its existence, assures us that it's harmless, that it isn't aiming for beauty or expressiveness or meaning, or even relevance.'

If entertainment in the cinema is unimportant then of course Miss Kael has a point. What she fails to acknowledge is that spoofing is often a form of homage (witness the Brooks films *High Anxiety* and *Young Frankenstein*) which, in view of the derivative nature of film-making as a whole, seems both legitimate and commend-able. Many of the so-called 'movie brats' of the new American cinema – Steven Spielberg, Brian De Palma, John Carpenter, John Landis, George Lucas et al – have been at pains to emulate their illustrious predecessors. Carpenter (*Halloween*, *The Fog*) and De Palma (*Carrie*, *Dressed to Kill*) have adopted, and occasionally extended, the masterly tricks of Hitchcock, while John Landis (*Kentucky Fried Movie*, *Animal House*, *An American Werewolf in London*) favours the ebullience and tastelessness of Mel Brooks. By experimenting with old techniques the novice becomes an innovator.

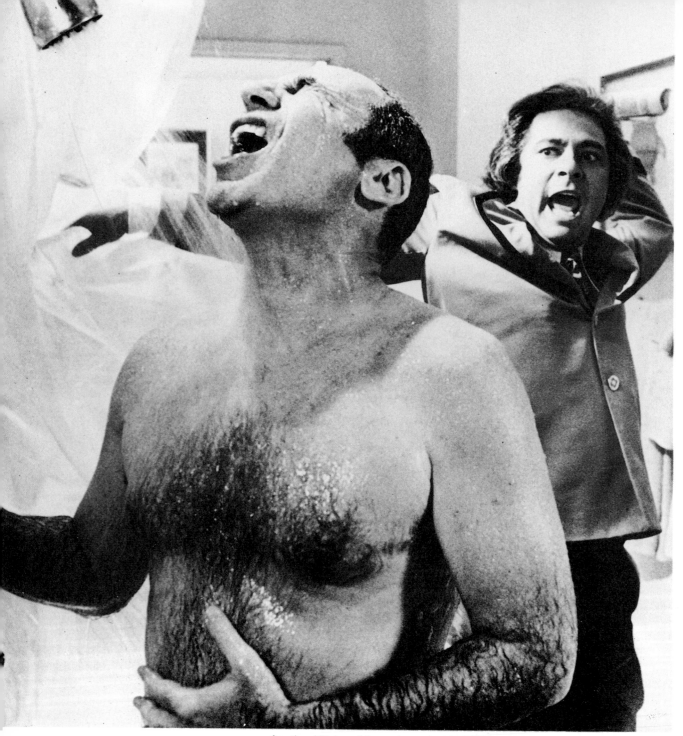

Another Hitchcock legend prepares to bite the dust.

Landis and co. proudly acknowledge their debt to directors and writers of the past whose work inspired and stimulated them as young men, just as the generation before them revered the pioneers of film comedy – Capra, Hawks, Lubitsch. As in all forms of culture, ideas and styles are passed down, recycled from generation to generation and there is sometimes a thin dividing line between the plagiarist and the adulator. Equally there is little to choose between the parasite and the parodist, except when it is clear that a spoof is motivated by affection rather than disdain.

Spoof is defined in the Oxford English Dictionary as slang for 'swindle or hoax' but in recent years it has become a synonym for parody or send-up. Clearly it was necessary to introduce a common denominator into the language for a style of comedy that has infiltrated and enlivened every form of popular entertainment. For all its transience and shallowness, the spoof is undoubtedly here to stay.

THE KAMINSKY KID

Funnymen through the ages have emerged from humble beginnings, giving substance to the belief that adversity is the mother of comic invention. Had the young Chaplin not grown up in the poorest streets of London, the world may never have known the poignant accuracy of his down-trodden little tramp. Had Minnie Schoenberg not badgered her four sons into forming a vaudeville act, we would have been denied the sublime lunacy of the Marx Brothers. Had Kate Kaminsky not given birth to a son, Melvin, in a Brooklyn tenement on June 28th 1926, 20th Century Fox would be millions of dollars the poorer.

The Kaminskys, first generation Russian immigrants, already had three sons – Irving, Lenny and Bernie – and the economic instability of this close-knit family became critical two years after Melvin's arrival with the sudden departure of his father, Max, aged 34, from kidney failure. Kate Kaminsky, a tiny woman of great spirit, found work in the knitting mills, and later on her two elder sons, Irving and Bernie, barely out of short trousers, dropped out of school to do menial jobs in the name of solvency. When Mel Brooks recalls his childhood it is not with a heavy heart or a furrowed brow.

'I was adored. I was always in the air, hurled up and kissed and thrown in the air again. Until I was six my feet didn't touch the ground. 'Look at those eyes! That nose! Those lips! That tooth! Get that child away from me quick, I'll eat him!' My mother was a true heroine. She was left with four boys and no income, so she got a job in the garment district. Worked the normal ten-hour day and then brought work home. All night she would sit up sewing, pressing rhinestones, going blind. Wonderful woman!'

If Mel Brooks inherited his mother's irrepressible zest for life – she is in her eighties now and living in Florida with her son's Oscar for *The Producers* – there is little doubt that his inclination to make jokes, whatever the circumstances or the company, derived from his grandmother, whose impenetrable accent made them incomprehensible to all but very close relatives.

On the streets of Williamsburg, the district where the Kaminskys lived, Melvin survived on his wits. It was a tough neighbourhood, polarized by immigrant groups – Irish, Polish, Italian, Jewish – and if your face didn't fit it was likely to be flattened. Fights were commonplace and abusive repartee was the accepted currency of communication. By comparison, life at home with the Kaminskys, fatherless as they were, was a perpetual bed of roses.

Ironically, the happiness of his childhood in Williamsburg backfired on the grown-up Brooks. He had such a difficult time adjusting to the decisions and responsibilities of adulthood that he spent six years undergoing psycho-analysis. He once described it as 'grieving about the death of childhood'. In the family home he'd always been the centre of attention, the court jester, the apple of his mother's eye. In trying to perpetuate these roles into adult life outside the family, he would often court hostility and bewilderment, rather than affection or acclaim. All performers want to be loved unreservedly, but anyone as wild and original as Brooks is sure to make enemies.

Brooks was no great scholar, being more eager to amuse his peers than impress his teachers. He was small, skinny and, by his own account, more like a Hebrew chipmunk than a human being. Laughter was the best form of defence. He became the class clown, a natural extension of his well-established role at home. The audience grew even wider when, at the age of 14, he took a bus ride into the Catskill Mountains and joined a stock company in the Borscht Belt – so called because the hotels are predominantly run and patronized by Jews.

In one play the precocious newcomer was cast as a 75-year-old lawyer, for which he was required to pour some water from a carafe and say: 'Here, have some water and calm down.'

'But on the opening night I'm a little nervous. So I dropped the carafe on the table, it smashed and made a waterfall off the table and all over the stage. The audience gasped. I don't waste a minute. I walk right down to the footlights, take off my grey toupee and say, 'I'm 14, what do you want?' Well I get a big laugh, but the director came running down the aisle and chased me through five Jewish resorts.'

Melvin's main job during the summer vacation was as a pool tummler, whose job it was to go out by the pool in the afternoon and keep the guests amused until the main entertainment of the evening. Brooks would attract their attention by walking off the end of the diving board, fully clothed and weighed down with suitcases. Desperate to make an impression he would contort his rubbery features into silly faces – anything for a laugh. Looking back, he admits it was dreadful, but his urge to succeed as an entertainer overcame any doubts he may have had about the future.

Patriotism was at its peak in 1944. Hearing of the Nazi atrocities against the Jews in Europe, Brooks enlisted in July of that year and after a short spell at the Virginia Military Institute he was sent to Fort Sill, Oklahoma, to train as a combat engineer. A few months later his unit was shipped off to Belgium where Brooks was actively involved in what later became known as The Battle of the Bulge. His job was to de-activate land mines ahead of the infantry – enough to wipe the smile off anyone's face. Brooks, however, still found time to fool around and claims the dubious distinction of being the only GI ever to serenade the Nazis with 'Toot-Toot-Tootsie'. The Germans had made a propaganda pitch by loudspeaker to his outfit, and Brooks responded with a heartfelt rendition of the Jolson number.

By the end of the war he was involved with army revues, entertaining the troops in occupied Germany and later at Fort Dix, New Jersey. The shows were raucous and outrageous, which suited Brooks fine. It was his first taste of the free-wheeling, improvised humour that was to become his staple diet over the next ten years.

Before the war, Brooks was taught to play the drums by a young friend name Buddy Rich, and on his return from Europe he decided to join a dance band at one of the Catskill resorts. Melvin Kaminsky didn't fit across the drum, so he changed his name to Melvin Brooks, a shortened version of his mother's maiden name, Brookman. When the resident comic went sick, the drummer was asked to lay aside his sticks and fill in.

'Here I am, I'm Melvin Brooks
I've come to stop the show
Just a ham who's minus looks

But in your hearts I'll grow
I'll tell you gags, I'll sing you songs
Just happy little snappy songs that roll along
Out of my mind, won't you be kind
And please love ... Melvin Brooks!'

Echoes of Gypsy Rose Lee's excrutiating 'Let Me Entertain You' ... only this precocious talent was nearly 20 and painfully aware that making people laugh was the only way he could earn a living, having decided to leave drumming to the incomparable Mr Rich. The middle-aged holiday-makers didn't know what to make of the pint-sized kid with the deep voice and anxious grin. 'We enjoyed certain parts of your show,' one well-wisher told him, 'but a trade would be better for you. Aviation mechanics are very well paid.'

'To begin with I did lousy jokes, any lousy joke would work. Then I decided to go out there and make up stuff. For instance, the manager where I was working, Pincus Cantor, an old-fashioned Jew from the Polish shtetl, he couldn't handle the loud speaker system at the hotel. He was never sure if he had the speaker off or on. It's a peaceful sunny day, people are snoozing in deck chairs, people are rowing across the lake. Suddenly a tremendous shout booms out: 'SON OF BITCH BASTARD! HOW DEY CAN LEAVE A SHEET SO FILT'Y! LET HIM SLEEP IN IT! I VUDN'T . . IT'S VAT? IT'S ON? OYYYYY!' Click. So I did Pincus Cantor on stage – big hit. But I wasn't a big hit, not at first. Usually I would be greeted by tumultuous yawns. The audience was between 65 and 85, that was rather a young audience for the mountains. They were more interested in their sponge cake and tea.'

Not only did the Borscht Belt provide Brooks with a comic apprenticeship, but it also brought him into contact with another Jewish comic whose talent gave Brooks an outlet for his own creative energy. It was laugh at first sight for Mel Brooks and Sid Caesar, an explosive marriage of wild imagination and dynamic interpretation. Like Brooks, Caesar began as a musician in the Catskills – he played saxophone with several different bands – but it soon became clear that his future lay in laughter. Brooks decided within days of meeting Caesar to give up his own aspirations as a performer and concentrate on providing material for a man he regarded as a comic genius. Though there is only a small age gap between them, Brooks was in awe of Caesar who lived up to his name. In appearance he was more akin to a matinee idol than a stand-up comic, being conventionally tall, dark and handsome. Together they must have looked as incongruous as Laurel and Hardy.

When Caesar was signed up for his own TV series, *Your Show of Shows*, he asked for Brooks to be recruited as a writer. But the show's producer, Max Liebman, had taken against Brooks, and Caesar was forced to commission gags and sketches from Brooks on the sly, paying for them out of his own pocket. Liebman soon realised the young writer's worth and took him on full-time. In less than a year, *Your Show of Shows* became the top-rating comedy show in America, 90 minutes every week, packed with comedy material of a quality seldom matched on American TV since. It paved the way for talents like Ernie Kovacs, Steve Allen and Jackie Gleason, and was the earliest forerunner to Rowan and Martin's *Laugh-In*, America's big comedy hit of the sixties.

At one time the team of writers on *Your Show of Shows* included Brooks, Neil and Danny Simon, Mel Tolkin, Larry Gelbart, Joe Stein and Woody Allen.

'Seven rats in a cage. In that room you had to fight to stay alive. Everybody hated everybody. We were all spoiled brats competing with each other for the king's favour, and we all wanted to come up with the funniest joke. I'd be damned if anybody would write anything funnier than I would, and everybody else felt the same way. The pitch sessions were lethal.'

Woody Allen remembers 'a high suffering quotient'. In those days he fancied himself as Ibsen and Brooks hankered after Dostoevski, although the prevailing mayhem worked against these somewhat esoteric aspirations. Allen, perhaps less introverted in his youth than he is now, still found the going rough. 'The atmosphere was one in which guys were shouting over one another, fighting to get their

lines heard.'

As if the strain of being funny six days a week (Sunday was the only day off) wasn't enough, Brooks was also called upon to play Sid Caesar's emotional nurse-maid, the only one on the team who knew how to defuse the star's black moods and temper tantrums. Brooks had such respect for Caesar — 'a massive talent, a messenger full of goodies' — that he was prepared to swallow his pride in the name of artistic temperament.

Brooks recalls the first sketch he wrote for Caesar — Jungle Boy — in which he plays a Tarzan-type character, raised by lions in Africa, who's been found walking the streets of New York.

Reporter: Sir, how do you survive in New York City?
Caesar: Survive?
Reporter: What do you eat?
Caesar: Pigeon.
Reporter: Don't the pigeons object?
Caesar: Only for a minute.
Reporter: What are you afraid of more than anything?
Caesar: Buick.
Reporter: You're afraid of a Buick?
Caesar: Yes, Buick can win in death struggle. Must sneak up on parked Buick, punch grille hard. Buick die.

The intense competition among the writers ensured that they gave their all, even if it wasn't always clear who was responsible for what. Material was selected on one basis only — was it funny enough to make the writing team laugh? If so, then the chances were that it would please the mighty Caesar. Besides, they found that even a less than brilliant sketch could come alive through his comic inventions.

Many sketches took the form of interviews, with Carl Reiner (better known these days as a film director) putting the questions. A particular favourite was the mad German professor with an extraordinary sense of logic and an accent you could cut with a knife. There was no Brooks character so bizarre that Caesar couldn't bring it to life with a semblance of plausibility. He managed to be convincing as a Freudian psychiatrist hotfoot from Vienna, a slot machine, a woman at her morning toilette, a bawling infant, and a British general.

Brooks thrived on the challenge of coming up with new characters and ideas every week. Everything he thought, felt and observed he regurgitated in comic form in order to meet the punishing TV schedule. He once estimated that he produced enough comedy material during the lifetime of *Your Show of Shows* to serve 25 feature films. Despite the pressure he did find time to get married, after a brief courtship, to a dancer named Florence Baum, attracted no doubt by his boundless energy and burgeoning bank balance.

For five years *Your Show of Shows* topped the ratings, and everyone involved became rich and nervous. Brooks was twenty five years old and earning 1,000 dollars a week, much to his amazement. In an interview with Playboy, he admitted that the pressure made him physically sick.

> 'I figured any day now they'd find me out and fire me. I used to vomit a lot between parked cars in midtown Manhattan. Sometimes I'd get so anxiety stricken I'd have to run, because I'd be generating too much adrenalin to do anything but run or scream. People stared. I couldn't sleep and I'd have dizzy spells.'

That kind of media success is short-lived, and it was the destructive egotism of Sid Caesar which brought the gravy train to a grinding halt at the dawn of the sixties. Brooks had just turned 30 and, with an ex-wife (his marriage to Florence Baum lasted six years) and three children to support, he found his income not so much reduced as extinguished.

Mel Brooks, you may have gathered, is not a man to sit around and sulk. True, the offers didn't come flooding in after the demise of his TV collaboration with Caesar, but Brooks made sure everyone knew he was around – and out of a job. Though he was widely regarded as a TV writer, Brooks was better known to his close friends as a frustrated performer, and now seemed a good opportunity to give vent to his natural instincts. Carl Reiner takes up the story.

> 'Mel was really using Caesar as a vehicle. What he secretly wanted was to perform himself. So in the evening we'd go to a party and I'd pick a character for him to play. I never told him what it was going to be, but I always tried for something that would force him to go into panic, because a brilliant mind in panic is a wonderful thing to see. For instance I might say, 'We have with us tonight the celebrated sculptor, Sir Jacob Epstone,' and he'd have to take it from there. Or I'd make him a Jewish pirate, and he'd complain about how he was being pushed out of the business because of the price of sailcloth and the cost of crews nowadays.'

One evening, after dinner at Reiner's home in Westchester, he chanced upon a character that was to become a minor cult figure in the States – the 2000 Year Old Man. 'Ladies and gentlemen,' he began, 'we are fortunate to have with us tonight, a man who was present at the crucifixion of Jesus Christ.'' Reiner then proceeded to quiz this improbable monument to longevity about his various historical acquaintances.

> Reiner: 'Did you know Jesus Christ?'
> Brooks: 'I knew him, I knew him. He was thin, he was nervous, wore sandals, came into the store, never bought anything. Asked for water, we gave him water. I didn't mind that he came into the store, but he always brought twelve guys with him.'

and later . . .

> Reiner: 'Sir, how many children do you have?'
> Brooks (with stoical self pity): 'I have over 42,000 children, and not one comes to visit.'

Joe Fields, the playwright, was responsible for introducing this unusual double act to people of influence, like Billy Rose and Moss Hart. Gradually they became talked about and sought after as a nighclub attraction. It was at Mamma Leone's, the trendy Manhattan restaurant, where the late Kenneth Tynan finally caught up with them. In addition to a favoured bunch of critics and columnists, the guest list included a selection of the show business celebrities then in New York, among them Claudette Colbert, Sam Goldwyn, John Gielgud, Ed Sullivan, Ethel Merman, Alec Guinness, Truman Capote and Marlene Dietrich. Tynan arrived late and found, not surprisingly, that it was standing room only.

'Peering over the heads of a hundred or so other standees, I saw two men in business suits. One, tall and lean, was conducting an interview with the other, who was short and compact. Their faces were among the few in the room which were not instantly recognisable. Though I took no notes, I recall much of what they said, and the waves of laughter that broke over it, and the wonder with which I realised that every word of it was improvised. When they stopped after about a quarter of an hour, the cabaret ended, and that was just as well, for nobody could have followed them. A crowd of professional entertainers erupted into cheers. The room buzzed with comment, yet hardly anyone seemed to know who the little maestro was. Diligent quizzing revealed that he was a 33-year-old television writer, that he had spent most of the preceding ten years turning sketches for Sid Caesar, and that his name was Mel Brooks. All I knew as I left Mamma Leone's that night was that he was the most original comic improviser I had ever seen.'

Inevitably, the 2,000 Year Old Man, and other improvisations, found their way into a recording studio before long, and they are still being reissued. There is also a cartoon version, which went out on release with *History of the World Part 1*. Sales of the record far exceeded Brooks's wildest expectations and helped him over a tricky financial patch. The record also led to a contract with Madison Avenue, doing improvised beer commercials with Dick Cavett, the talk show host, acting as a Reiner-type feed. This suited the Brooks style perfectly, relying on the momentary flash of inspiration, rather than hours of sweated labour at the typewriter.

Brooks and Cavett were given a completely free hand by the advertising agency, enabling them to fly off at imaginative tangents. The sessions would be punctuated at regular intervals by Cavett's uncontrollable giggles – usually inspired by a stream of mock abuse from Brooks, who described him as the most gentile person he'd ever seen. Brooks had no qualms about exploiting the 2,000 Year Old Man for commercial purposes. He was still out of a regular job at this time, and Madison Avenue

wooed him with the kind of offer he could not afford to refuse.

'I decided that I'd given enough of myself to mankind. After all my definitive 12-volume series on penology was completed, my staff and I had UNESCO running in apple pie order, and of course I'd just come up with the vaccine to wipe out cystic fibrosis. So I felt I could afford to allow myself a few monetary indulgences.'

After ten years of frenzied performing in a small smoke-filled room to an audience of hyper-critical writers, all competing with one another, Brooks welcomed the opportunity to unleash his improvisational talent on an unsuspecting public – and suddenly everyone was talking about *that beer commercial*, as if it was some exciting new concept in comedy, which in a way it was. Chat show hosts were falling over themselves to get Mel Brooks; rarely does a new talent emerge who talks as much as Brooks, or as wittily. Ever the show off, Brooks revelled in the attention and acclaim, but he was still anxious to get back into the mainstream of TV comedy. The original idea for *Get Smart* came from producers David Susskind and Dan Melnick, who brought in Brooks and another talented young writer, Buck Henry, to develop it into a situation comedy for the ABC network.

Henry, who went on to write the screenplays for *The Graduate*, *Catch 22* and *What's Up Doc?*, soon adjusted to the Brooks style of script-acting, in which the typewriter is largely redundant, and what emerged was a wild parody of the spy genre, as popularized by James Bond and *The Man from UNCLE*, featuring an agent called Maxwell Smart, who confounds the enemy not with any futuristic gadgetry or muscular prowess, but simply by his own stupidity.

Situation comedy up to that time was consistently insipid, and the powers that be at ABC decided that *Get Smart* was too wide a departure from that tradition. It just wasn't cosy enough. Henry and Brooks tried to meet them half-way by including a dog as Smart's sidekick, but ABC felt this would offend dog lovers, as the dog was asthmatic and even dumber than its owner.

Public smiles as Mr & Mrs. Brooks face the cameras together.

Soon after the project was abandoned by ABC, a rival network, NBC, picked it up and the show became a huge nationwide success, appealing to viewers of all ages. It was something completely different, a sitcom based on the wild exploits of an idiot, with no claims to realism and no sanctimonious pay-off. Brooks was particularly pleased with the way Don Adams developed the role of Smart, with his piggy eyes and self satisfied smirk, always one step behind his far brighter accomplice, Agent 99, played by the delectable Barbara Feldon. There were frequent cries of bad taste – one episode about a fat man kidnapped by Smart's adversaries was entitled Survival of the Fattest – but the writers rarely sucumbed to pressure from the NBC executives. As far as Brooks was

concerned, bad taste was an essential comedy component, as he was soon to demonstrate with unfettered zeal.

By this time he was married again – to the actress Anne Bancroft, whom he met and fell madly in love with at a recording of The Perry Como Show in 1961. Bancroft was riding high at the time, having won awards for Broadway appearances in *Two for the Seesaw* and *The Miracle Worker*.

On meeting her for the first time, Brooks' opening gambit is reputed to be: 'Hi, I'm Mel Brooks . . I'd *kill* for you!' Physically, it seemed an odd match. For all his virtues, Brooks is no Adonis and socially he is often overbearing, while Bancroft comes over as beautiful, bright and worldly. But the more they came to know

Director Brooks lines up a shot on the set of Blazing Saddles.

each other, the more alike they found themselves. Like Brooks, Bancroft was the daughter of poor immigrants, Italians living in the Bronx. In a large family she had always been the one called upon to amuse the others, so becoming an actress seemed like a natural progression from childhood exhibitionism.

Professionally they were alike too. Neither had succeeded in combining a happy love life with a busy career, so both tended to concentrate all their energy on the latter. But as their devotion to each other grew, all that started to change. They became inseparable, and when Bancroft went to England to appear in the film *The Pumpkin Eater*, Brooks flew across the Atlantic every other weekend for three months, ignoring his aversion to flying.

At the time of their marriage in 1964, Bancroft was a lot more famous than Brooks, having won the previous year an Oscar for her brilliant performance as Annie Sullivan in *The Miracle Worker*. As if to redress the balance, Brooks part-won an Oscar in 1964 for writing and narrating a cartoon short called *The Critic*, a wry comment on modern art as perceived by a disappointed voyeur.

Together they made an illustrious couple and Brooks was always proud to be seen with his glamorous wife on public ocasions. He was no less proud of her achievements as an actress and it was probably the competitive streak in him which brought about a gradual reassessment of his own professional status.

For some time he had felt constricted by the rigours of network TV. They flattered him and promised him creative freedom, but he knew from past experience that a script for TV ceases to be yours as soon as you let it out of your sight. Ever the perfectionist, Brooks felt he had earned the right to control the fate of his creative labours.

Like all writers for the media, Brooks had aspirations to more serious and durable writing. For years he had been telling people at parties that he was working on a novel about Hitler and Eva Braun. Being Brooks, however, the only serious thing about it was the po-faced way he responded to earnest inquiries about this imaginary work of high literary art. What he did consider in a more serious light was the prospect of adapting this idea to the cinema – a medium he felt would be more conducive to his quest for autonomy.

19

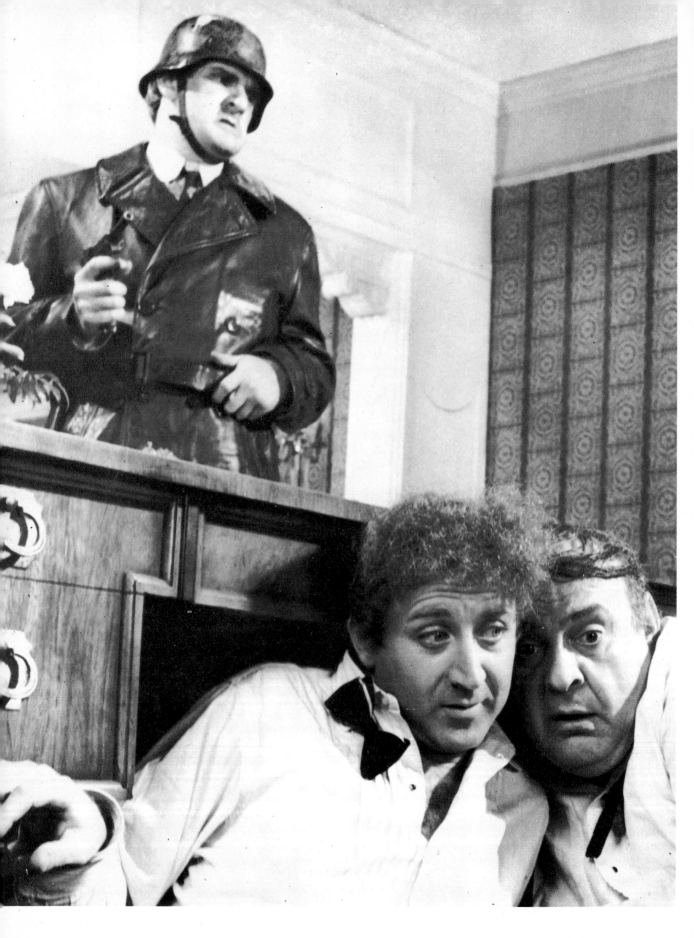

Liebkin (Kenneth Mars), appalled by the treatment of his
hymn to Hitler, tracks down the culprits in The Producers.

FUNNY IS IN THE WRITING

Hitler had always been a popular target of derision on *Your Show of Shows* and stand up comics like Will Jordan and Lenny Bruce had evolved Hitler routines as part of their act. But in 1966 nobody had yet come up with a hippie Hitler as the centrepiece of a musical extravaganza. Indeed nobody in their right mind would consider it, which is precisely why it appealed to Mel Brooks as the key sequence of *The Producers*. He needed a subject that was in such poor taste that the producers of the title, having raised vast amounts of money from elderly female backers, could then abscond with the cash when the show proved to be a monumental flop.

Like most professional writers, Brooks was loath to waste time on a project without some firm assurance that it would eventually come to fruition. The problem was finding a real life producer willing to bear the fruit, and someone who would allow Brooks to direct. Not that he was specially anxious to become another Frank Capra, but he felt it was the only way to protect and safeguard his material.

Sidney Glazier, award-winning producer of *The Eleanor Roosevelt Story*, fell about when

Brooks enacted *The Producers* in his office. He knew the risks – Brooks was untried and hotheaded – but Glazier's admiration of his writing and performing talent gave the confidence to trust his hunch. He raised 600,000 dollars and another 500,000 was put up by Joseph E. Levine, head of Embassy Pictures, for the distribution rights.

Brooks agreed to a cut-price fee to keep the costs down, but only if Levine would forego 'the right of final cut', by which the distributor can call in an outsider after the film is finished to do a little cosmetic surgery if he feels the film isn't going to sell on its own merits. Needless to say, this is anathema to perfectionist film directors and Brooks remained adamant on this point until Levine reluctantly conceded.

It is indicative of the faith Mel Brooks had in *The Producers* (not to mention himself) that he'd come all this way without actually producing a script. Much as he enjoys writing and generating laughter, the prospect of shutting himself away for months on end to create the masterpiece he knew everyone was expecting did not hold any joy for him.

He missed the instant feedback of collaborators, the competitive spirit of TV writing, and the love-hate relationships that inspired him in fallow periods. For all his creative zeal, Brooks lacks the introspection and solitude of a natural writer. It took nine months of painful application to complete the script, but it was nine months well spent. It is undoubtedly one of the most inventive comedy film scripts ever written and deservedly won the 1968 Oscar for best original screenplay.

Those of us for whom the film has become a cult found lines of dialogue becoming part of our everyday lives. 'If you got it, flaunt it'. . . 'I'm wet and I'm hysterical'. . . 'Hitler could paint an apartment in one afternoon, two coats.' Lines that mean nothing to the uninitiated take on a life of their own, even out of context.

Long before he started to think seriously about making the film, Brooks had two actors in mind for the roles of Max Bialystock and Leo Bloom, the two Jewish producers of the title who team up to present 'a surefire flop' (viz 'Springtime for Hitler') with a view to making off with all the backers' money.

For Bloom, the nervous young accountant who falls under Bailystock's spell, Brooks wanted Gene Wilder, then unknown, whose only other film experience had been a small but noticeable character part in *Bonnie and Clyde*. He worked on stage with Anne Bancroft in Brecht's *Mother Courage* and had come to know the couple as friends. Even so, Wilder was astonished when Brooks turned up out of the blue, years after the role of Bloom was first offered, and asked if he was still interested. Brooks told him he wouldn't have to act at all because he was so much like the character of Bloom – timid, vulnerable, self effacing. In short, frightened of Life.

Interestingly, the father-son relationship between Bialystock and Bloom in the film closely mirrored the off-screen relationship between Brooks and Wilder, which helped the latter strengthen his confidence, to the extent that he now writes and directs his own movies. The resilience shown by Mel Brooks after the collapse of Caesar's empire, and his continuing lack of critical favour in the face of commercial success, has been a source of inspiration to Wilder.

Casting Bialystock, the seedy, unscrupulous impresario, was not quite so simple. Brooks knew whom he wanted – Zero Mostel – but the big Broadway star of *Fiddler on the Roof* and *A Funny Thing Happened on the Way to the Forum* had strong reservations. 'What's this,' he bellowed on first reading the script, 'a Jewish producer going to bed with old women on the brink of the grave? I can't play such a part, it's sick.'

With the connivance of Mostel's wife, Brooks finally managed to coax him into it, and the reluctance with which Mostel accepted the role no doubt accounted for the tempestuous relationship between director and star on the set. Brooks described it as 'like working in the middle of a thunderstorm' and Mostel resented the demands made of him. 'That man is going to kill me', he'd scream as Brooks called for the umpteenth take.

But out of chaos and conflict came one of the most inspired performances in the history of film comedy, a virtuoso display of grotesque comic artistry by a man whose features had the mobility of a water bed and the expressiveness of a precocious child. Mostel's early scenes with Gene Wilder, when neither Bialystock nor Bloom is sure of each other's sanity, combine the physical delicacy of a Laurel and Hardy routine with the verbal dexterity of Abbott and Costello. Like all the best double acts, they complemented each other in terms of personality and outlook, as well as size. Armed with a battery of vintage Brooks one-liners, two such consummate comic actors could hardly fail to ignite.

Originally Brooks himself intended to play the role of Franz Liebkin, the mad German responsible for 'Springtime for Hitler', but Kenneth Mars caused such a sensation when he read for it that the writer-director wisely decided to give Mars a break and stay out of the limelight. If Bialystock is larger than life, Liebkin is twice as ugly, a cartoon Nazi, complete with helmet, mad accent and Hitler fixation. When he sees what the producers have done to his beloved Führer, Liebkin's first reaction is to descend on their office and shoot the slanderers dead. Ever the survivor, Bialystock persuades the trigger-happy lunatic that the real culprits are the company and

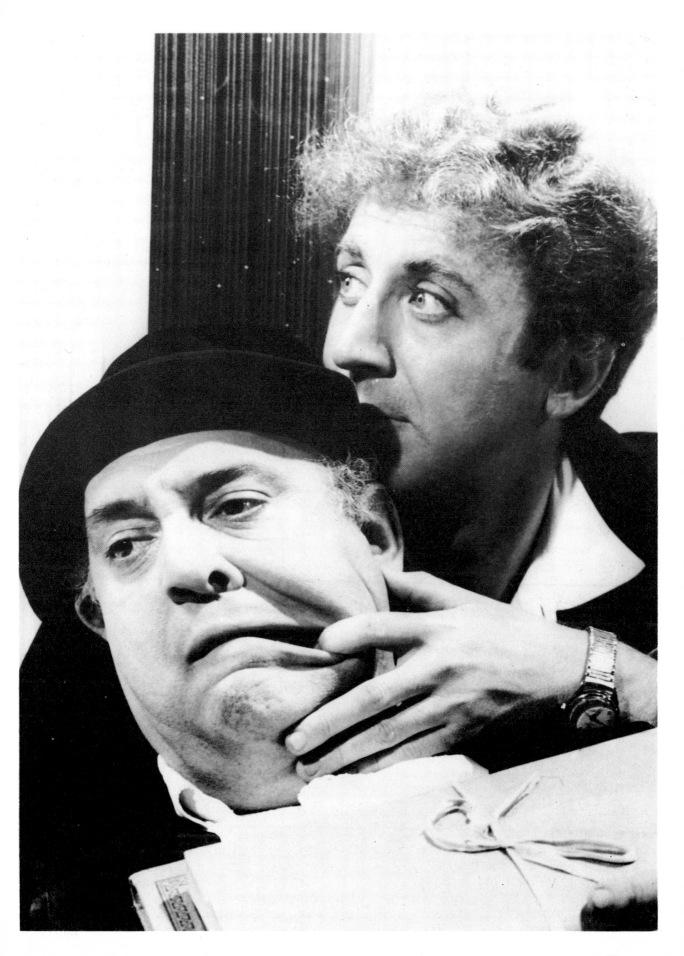

Bialystock and Bloom suffer Franz Liebkin's Nazi repertoire in The Producers.

Bialystock (Zero Mostel) is floored by one of his geriatric backers.

that he'd achieve a more lasting retribution by blowing up the theatre. By Bialystock's twisted logic, this would also solve the problem of the show's commercial success, which took the fraudulent couple totally by surprise.

The Producers opened in 1968 to mixed reviews. Critics, on the whole, recognised its originality and fine performances, but accused Brooks of over-statement, self-indulgence, and inconsistency. 'It ends in a whimper of sentimentality out of keeping with the low jinks that went before,' wrote the reviewer for Time magazine.

In another review, Andrew Sarris of Village Voice dismissed Brooks's directing as 'thoroughly vile and inept . . . everyone in the film mugs with an extravagance not seen since the most florid silent days.'

At a time when American film comedy was represented by The Odd Couple, an immaculate Neil Simon play cleverly transferred to the screen, and The Graduate, a sophisticated, well structured blend of realistic humorous observation and fictional romanticism, there were no stylistic pigeon holes into which a Jewish maverick like Brooks would comfortably fit, hence the general feeling of discomfort among the more serious and self-regarding critics.

Only Wanda Hale of the Daily News lavished on The Producers the kind of praise every first-time director craves, describing it as 'a fantasy with profound undertones . . . sheer magic.' But one cheer doesn't make an ovation and Brooks was deeply hurt by the kind of critical antipathy he'd never experienced before. Why, he wondered, should they take such a hard line when all he wanted was to make people laugh? It was as if certain films, regardless of their intentions, were doomed to be sacrificed before the altar of critical consensus.

In an attempt to redress the balance, Peter Sellers took full page advertisements in two West Coast newspapers, extolling the film's virtues in conversely extravagant terms:

Last night I saw the ultimate film, The Producers, brilliantly written and directed by Mel Brooks. It is the essence of all great comedy combined in a single motion picture. Without any doubt Mel Brooks displays true genius in weaving together tragedy-comedy, comedy-tragedy, pity, fear, hysteria, schizophrenia, inspired madness and a largesse of lunacy with sheer magic.'

There was a rumour at the time that Brooks had written the commendation himself and simply asked Sellers to put his name to it. Either way, it had the desired effect and the film covered its

Ron Moody gets more than he bargained for – namely Dom DeLuise in drag – in The Twelve Chairs.

Will his chair contain a fortune . . . Dom DeLuise is about to find out.

Frank Langella looks on while Mel Brooks and Ron Moody rehearse a scene from The Twelve Chairs.

production costs five times over in its first year, and within two years had attained a cult status on both sides of the Atlantic.

If *The Producers* made a penny, Mel Brooks is fond of saying, his next film, *The Twelve Chairs*, made a halfpenny. It was a commercial flop on such a scale as to make his survival in the film world little short of miraculous. Brooks had dreamed of making *The Twelve Chairs* – based on a classic Russian novel by Ilf and Petrov – since he was first captivated by Russian literature in his teens. It is set in 1927 and concerns the quest of a lapsed nobleman, played by Ron Moody, for his family jewels which reside in the seat of a gold brocade dining chair (one of a set) long since appropriated by the Communist authorities. He is aided and hindered respectively by a conniving priest (Dom DeLuise) and a deceitful young charmer, played by Frank Langella, more recently seen as Dracula.

No longer able to resist the lure of the lights, Brooks cast himself in the small but noticeable role of the aristocrat's former serf, now caretaker of an old people's home. He had no illusions about who was to blame if the film didn't work. 'Listen, I wrote it, directed it, acted in it and composed the title song,' he told English journalist Lee Langley at the time, 'If I could I'd usher people into their seats, I care so much about it. On the surface it's wild comedy, then underneath it deals with human greed and governmental stupidity, and pervading every-thing the vapour of the Russian soul.'

The vapour of the Russian soul? Was this the same guy who turned Hitler into a song and dance man? The fact was that Brooks sought to break the mould wherein *The Producers* had cast him, and emerge as the funnyman with a message. He looked upon *The Twelve Chairs* as a pathway to critical acceptance and credibility.

To give the film an authentic look and to save money, Brooks decided to shoot it in Yugoslavia, keeping the budget to a minimal 1.4 million dollars. The country also yielded a first-rate cinematographer, Djordje Nilolic, who ensured that at least the film would look good.

Other than that, Yugoslavia was not a place where Mel Brooks would choose to hang his hat for any longer than necessary:

'When I went to Yugoslavia, my hair was black . . . when I came back, nine months later, it was grey. Truly. To begin with, it's a very long flight and you land in a field of full grown corn. They figure it cushions the landing. At night you can't do anything because all of Belgrade is lit by a 10 watt bulb, and you can't go anywhere because Tito has the car. The food is either very good or very bad. One day we arrived on location late and starving and they served us fried chains. When we got to our hotel rooms, mosquitoes as big as George Foreman were waiting for us. They were sitting in armchairs with their legs crossed.'

For those who felt that *The Producers* was the work of a comic genius, *The Twelve Chairs* came as a crushing disappointment. It had its moments, of course, but for the most part it was overplayed and undernourished. Brooks aimed for a fusion of his own manic comedy with the simplistic Russian satire, but the result seemed to confirm what its detractors had said of *The Producers* – that Brooks lacked the objectivity and discipline of a great comic imagination.

New York critics seemed generally agreed on the film's one outstanding asset – Mel Brooks' performance as the demented serf – although Vincent Canby of the New York Times resented his desire 'to be lovable and stamp on your foot at the same time'. Pauline Kael felt the subject matter gave Brooks 'an opportunity to show his nostalgic affection for the slapstick and mugging and innocent nuttiness of earlier periods.'

Few denied it was a bold choice of subject, coming after *The Producers*, and the writer-director was admired within the business for his tenacity in the face of box office disaster. It was, however, a recklessness that almost cost him a career in the film business, and Brooks soon came to realise that a director is only as viable as his box office returns.

The Twelve Chairs died on both sides of the Atlantic – many confirmed Brooks fans have never heard of it to this day – and its creator resolved to look around for a more commercial property. 'There is no room in the business for a special little picture,' he reflected in a press interview, 'you either hit 'em over the head, or stay home with the canary.'

KING OF THE SPOOFERS

Failure is tantamount to a bad smell in America and failure in the film business is an unacceptable stench. In 1970, at the age of 44, Mel Brooks was regarded by the industry and, worse still, by himself as a failure. Like success, failure can be self perpetuating and his next idea for a movie spelled F-L-O-P to all but the short-sighted perpetrator. He had seen and been impressed by an off-Broadway production of *She Stoops to Conquer*. It struck him as 'Mozartean' and he promptly set about adapting it for the screen, the idea being that Albert Finney, whom he had admired so much in *Tom Jones*, would play Tony Lumpkin. He knew that he, in turn, was much admired by Finney, whose record of the 2,000 Year Old Man was among his most prized possessions. Finney was excited at the prospect of working with such a talent, but he felt there was no commercial sense in a film of *She Stoops to Conquer*. Brooks met with the same response from agents, producers and studios. They were all agreed it was just another surefire flop.

A full two years after *The Twelve Chairs*, Brooks had a chance encounter with David Begelman, vice chairman of an influential talent agency (and subsequently head of Columbia Pictures) that was to alter the course of his career. Brooks, down on his luck like never before, needed little persuasion to take advantage of Begelman's offer to represent him ('You're nobody and I'm everybody . . . it's a good deal,' said the agent, according to Brooks). Soon after, Brooks received a call from Warner Brothers asking if he'd be interested in re-writing a treatment of a comedy western entitled Tex-X by Andrew Bergman. He demurred, but sent the treatment to Begelman for his opinion. Again according to Brooks, their discussion over the treatment that was to cure all his ills, went as follows:

Begelman: I think this could be very funny. Do you want to do it?
Brooks: No.
Begelman: All right, you don't want to do it. Fine. You'll do it.
Brooks: Why do I have to do it?
Begelman: Because you owe a fortune in alimony, because you are in debt, and

The only Jewish Indian chief in Hollywood . . . Mel Brooks groans under the weight of make-up and feathers in Blazing Saddles.

*Business is slack for the sherriff (Cleavon Little) and his
deputy (Gene Wilder) in Blazing Saddles.*

because you have no choice. You have to do
it, and with all the talent you possess.
Brooks: OK, I'll do it . . . as long as I can have
Andrew Bergman to work with.
Begelman: I'll make that one of the conditions.
Brooks: I want to do it the way we did *Your
Show of Shows*. We'll get a black writer,
maybe Richard Pryor, and a comedy team,
like Norman Steinberg and Alan Uger, and
we'll lock ourselves up and write it together,
fancy-free and crazy.

Pryor was assigned to write the Jewish jokes,
and the Jews would write the black jokes. Brooks
envisaged a surrealist epic aimed at two weirdos
in the balcony. 'It was time to take two eyes, the
way Picasso had done it, and put them on one
side of the nose, because the official movie
portrait of the West was simply a lie. I figured my
career was finished anyway, so I wrote berserk,

heartfelt stuff about white corruption and racism
and Bible-thumping bigotry.'

Frustrated for so long by failure and indif-
ference (other people's that is), Brooks purged
himself in nine months of creative incubation at
the end of which he gave mirth in the form of
Blazing Saddles. It was just like old times. The
reason it took so long for five writers to produce
one script is that the first draft provided enough
material for an eight-hour movie, so they had to
go back and embark on the painful process of
editing their own script.

Meanwhile Warner Brothers agreed to let
Brooks direct, with Michael Hertzberg
producing. Cleavon Little was signed to play the
black dude whose only hope of escaping the
hangman's noose is by agreeing to become
sheriff of Rock Ridge – a small township
terrorised by a gang of land grabbers in the
employ of a crooked lawyer called Hedley

Lamarr. Lamarr, whose name is constantly mispronounced so as to sound like the 1930s film star, knows that the arrival of a black sheriff will throw the bigoted inhabitants of Rock Ridge into even further turmoil. Indeed the new sheriff is driven to holding himself hostage in order to escape being lynched on arrival by the so-called welcoming party — surely one of the film's more surreal conceits.

Little's performance is cool, cute and low-key, as is Gene Wilder in the supporting role of The Waco Kid, a disillusioned gunfighter who claims to have killed more men than Cecil B. DeMille. In contrast, the other key performances are at the broad end of the comedy spectrum: Harvey Korman as the transparently evil Lamarr, Madeline Kahn as the man-eating Lilli von Shtupp, and Brooks himself as the cross-eyed, girl-hungry Governor William J. LePetomane, who seems to have stepped straight out of a Marx Brothers movie, but without the benefit of Groucho's whiplash wit. By some extraordinary oversight, Brooks created a plum part for himself and then forgot to give the character anything funny to say!

After nearly a year on the movie, they were ready to screen a rough assembly for the top brass at Warner Brothers, in the sure knowledge that they were handing over a hit. But the screening proved to be more of an indictment than a confirmation. At the end the studio executives filed out in grim silence and Brooks knew he was finished. Producer Michael Hertzberg had seen this reaction before, however, and resolved to give the film a public trial before any executions took place.

Hertzberg set up a preview that evening in a larger theatre and invited secretaries, janitors, waiters, anyone but studio chiefs. By the evening word had got around that it was a stinker, because of the earlier fiasco, so the audience of 240 was quiet and wary. The credits began to roll and Frankie Laine struck up the rousing title song. A few chuckles, sympathy perhaps. Then the railroad sequence, where the sadistic overseer demands 'a good old nigger work song' from his black chain gang — and Cleavon Little breaks into 'I get no kick from champagne', the ultra sophisticated Cole Porter number beloved of Sinatra and Tony Bennett. From then on the laughter never stopped. 'It was like a Chagall painting,' said a fanciful Brooks, 'people left their chairs and floated upside down.'

Neither did the laughter stop when the film was let loose on the film-going public of America. Brooks claimed to have made 'an esoteric little picture' for film buffs, sending up every western cliché in the book, but he seemed to forget that the western was a way of life for the vast majority of Americans — and a spoof as rich and fulsome as Blazing Saddles could hardly fail to spark a reaction. As Kenneth Tynan remarked, it is low comedy in which many of the custard pies are camouflaged hand grenades. The jokes are about as subtle as a force nine gale, and one of them produced a comparable blast of wind. When asked the point of the farting scene, in which cowboys let off steam after a surfeit of beans, Mel Brooks replied: 'The farts were the point of the farting scene.' Point taken.

Brooks came in for a lot of criticism over the portrayal of Mongo, a cretin of formidable strength, who fells a horse with a swift right-hander. The New York Times published a protest letter from the father of a retarded child, accusing Brooks of perpetuating the concept of the mental defective as clown. Books was not as immune to charges of bad taste then as he is now, and that one hurt him more than most.

It is difficult to see why the hierarchy of Warner Brothers had quite such a negative reaction. Every other frame is bursting with bad taste — or what is conventionally regarded as bad taste — from the preacher who talks about 'jerking off' to the Dietrich-type chanteuse with a speech impediment. I need hardly say that Brooks eschews the conventions of good and bad taste. In a world that finds rape and murder acceptable means of entertainment in such films as Death Wish and Dirty Harry, scatological indulgence seems a petty crime by comparison.

The reason *Blazing Saddles* went on to become one of the most successful ever film comedies is that its humour has a common denominator, albeit low, in simple vulgarity. Even the most sophisticated among us is prey to the absurdities and indignities of human behaviour and, to Mel Brooks, the denial of dignity is there to be exploited.

Nowhere does *Blazing Saddles* part company with the conventions of taste, sanity or the cinema itself more blatantly than in the gloriously chaotic finale, where the entire company bursts through the set of a musical extravaganza under the direction of an ultra-camp Dom DeLuise, leading to an incongruous brawl between actors in cowboy gear and a bunch of mincing Fred Astaire look-alikes. In the ensuing mayhem Cleavon Little ducks out to Grauman's Chinese Theatre, which just happens to be showing a movie called, er, *Blazing Saddles*.

Even before the film was released, Brooks was beginning to think like a winner again. In the past he'd been dependent on the approval and acclaim of his peers in television and the movies, but from now on he would look to the public, and box office returns, for his adrenalin. The decision to make his next film, *Young Frankenstein*, in black and white shows just how confident he must have been feeling – and the high esteem in which he was held by the executives of Twentieth Century Fox, delighted of course that he'd defected from Warner Brothers.

The idea for a Frankenstein spoof was actually Gene Wilder's. Legend has it that Brooks asked Wilder to play The Waco Kid at the last minute (the actor who was originally cast having dropped out) and Wilder agreed on condition that Brooks would collaborate with him on *Young Frankenstein*. Wilder wrote the first draft when *Blazing Saddles* was in production, and then he and Brooks got together on the final draft. It was a speedy and harmonious partnership, despite their often contrasting views on film comedy.

'Mel will take a shotgun with fifty pellets in it,' explains Wilder, 'and fifteen miss the target while another fifteen hit the outside rim. Ten more hit nearer to the centre, and ten are right on the bulls-eye. I take a high-powered rifle, a steady aim, and try to hit the centre. It may be a fault and it may be a virtue, I don't know.'

The effect of one on the other was highly beneficial. Wilder restrained Brooks, who in turn liberated Wilder, with the result that the jokes evolved out of the narrative, rather than the other way round as in *Blazing Saddles*. Also, the characters appear more three-dimensional, so that Marty Feldman's occasional asides to camera (as Igor, of the moveable hump) seem out of place. In fact you can almost divide the film into Brooks scenes and Wilder scenes in terms of indulgence and restraint. Like the monster created by Baron von Frankenstein's genial grandson, the film is made up of misappropriated parts. Both Brooks and Wilder are lifelong fans of the horror-monster genre, and hardcore buffs have a wonderful time spotting the references, some intentional, some inadvertent. 'Pardon me boy, is this the Transylvania Station,' shouts Frankenstein as the train grinds to a halt. 'Yeah,' says a boy in lederhosen, 'Track 29.' Brooks adores running jokes and, to the continuing irritation of film critics, they have become a familiar feature of his work. *Young Frankenstein* contains at least half a dozen, among them Igor's itinerant hump, which he refuses to acknowledge; the local police chief's impenetrable accent; and the untouchability of Young Frankenstein's fiancée (Madeline Kahn) who is finally bowled over by the rapacious monster. Then there is the formidable house-keeper, Frau Blücher, the very mention of whose name unfailingly prompts a chorus of nervous whinnies from the stables. Considering how few funny lines she has, this is a rich comic caricature by Cloris Leachman, whose first appearance it was with the Brooks repertory.

What gives the film its essential vein of pathos – apart from Gerald Hirschfeld's atmospheric photography and some superb mood music – is Peter Boyle's monster, a simple soul in torment, so comical in the song and dance number with his master (the most inspired comic sequence of any Brooks film to date) and so tragic in the scene with Gene Hackman's blundering blind man. Thanks to the credibility of Boyle's performance and the intensity of Wilder's the narrative holds together and for once Brooks the anarchist isn't allowed to eclipse Brooks the ranconteur.

In an attempt to legitimise himself in the eyes

of certain American critics – or maybe just to have fun at their expense – Brooks started to intellectualise the film, calling Frankenstein's mission 'a challenge to God . . . the quest to defeat death'. He also talked about 'womb envy' as the theme of Mary Shelley's original story, the frustration of man's inability to give life, which may well account for Frankenstein's continuing fascination and popularity.

Such reflections, while showing him to be more than a wise-cracking clown, cut no ice with the film-going public who flocked to *Young Frankenstein* because it was inventive, undemanding escapism – a formula that is a lot older and every bit as durable as the legend itself.

With two substantial hits under his belt, Brooks confounded colleagues and critics alike in 1975 by announcing his return to TV. He would collaborate as writer with producer Norman Steinberg on a spoof series about Robin Hood and his merry men, to be called *When Things Were Rotten*. As in *Blazing Saddles*, the idea was to exploit the period setting and characters in terms of contemporary dialogue and

conventions. But the razor sharp gagster of *Your Show of Shows* and *Get Smart* had matured into an all-rounder whose talent was now more evenly spread over a wider canvas. In other words, the show didn't work. 'It's bizarre, not funny,' pronounced one critic in the Wall Street Journal. Brooks's hard-won success in the movies didn't count for much on the small screen, and the critics were quick to draw attention to an already conspicuous TV comeback.

Far from downhearted, Brooks threw himself into his most daring project to date, one that was considered positively suicidal by many studio executives at the time. Namely, *Silent Movie*. The notion of Mel Brooks, known and revered for his narrative wit and spontaneity, making a film with no words, seemed as perverse as Mohommad Ali refusing to throw punches in a title fight. Clearly Brooks was trying to prove to himself and everyone else that he could be funny without ever uttering a word. He was also putting the Green Awning Syndrome to the test. For the uninitiated, the Green Awning Syndrome refers to the tendency of the big studios to put money

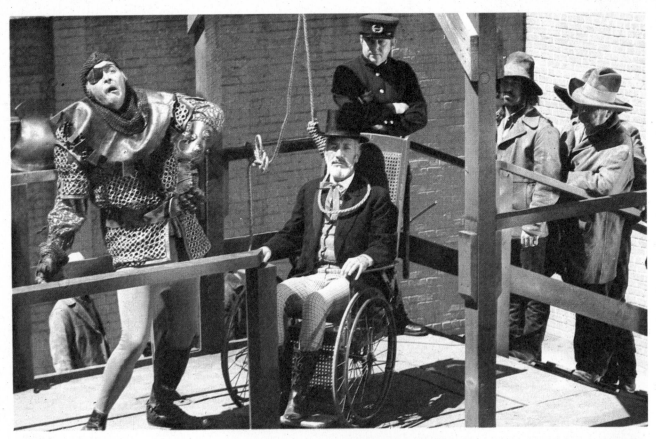

Top: Someone's in the wrong film, or is this Blazing
Saddles?
Bottom: Mel Brooks the director confronts Peter Boyle the
monster in Young Frankenstein.

*Cloris Leachman as the fearsome Frau Blucher snubs Igor
(Marty Feldman) in Young Frankenstein.*

Marty Feldman as the abominable Igor (pronounced Eye-gore) in Young Frankenstein.

*Mel Brooks comes on like Cecil B. DeMille on the set of
Silent Movie.*

into any project suggested by producers in favour – even if the idea strikes them, as *Silent Movie* must have, as being commercially unsound.

Presumably the top brass of Twentieth Century Fox, thinking of the huge success of *Blazing Saddles* and *Young Frankenstein*, were scared Brooks would take the idea to another studio if they turned him down. He offered some consolation by promising guest appearances by Paul Newman, Liza Minelli, Burt Reynolds, James Caan and his wife, Anne Bancroft. The only person to speak would be the French mime, Marcel Marceau, uttering a resonant 'Non' down the phone.

Brooks himself would play the leading role of Mel Funn, a film director trying to set up a silent movie in order to save a small studio, Sunshine Films, from being taken over by the multi-national conglomerate, Engulf and Devour. In his quest for Hollywood stars to appear in his films, Funn enlists the help of an incongruous duo – Dom DeLuise and Marty Feldman – and the three of them drive around in a tiny sports car.

Even more so than *Blazing Saddles*, *Silent Movie* comprises a series of set pieces, with the appropriate captions and incidental music. Though there is a narrative of sorts, it matters about as much as in a Laurel and Hardy film, where all the enjoyment is in the inter-action of two consummate blunderers. Likewise Brooks, Feldman and DeLuise are constantly getting in each other's way and disgracing themselves in public. In paying homage to the great comics of the silent era, Brooks made a virtue out of simplicity. The film proved as accessible to audiences in Timbuctu as it was to the more sophisticated moviegoers of Los Angeles, and there is every reason to believe it gave more pleasure to the former than the latter. For all his literary pretensions, Brooks is pimarily concerned with entertaining his audience by whatever means are most easily assimilated by the largest number of people.

From the universal concept of *Silent Movie*, Brooks turned his now ravenous eye to an altogether more local genre – the Hitchcock thriller – but in such a way as to make it entertaining and comprehensible to those unfamiliar with *Psycho*, *Vertigo*, *The Birds*, *North by Northwest*

Guess who tore the leg off the doll in Young Frankenstein?

Wilder, Kahn, Feldman and Brooks discuss the next scene
during the shooting of Young Frankenstein.

A flock of incontinent pigeons moves in for the kill in *High Anxiety*.

and *Spellbound*, all of which provided source material for this sporadically hilarious spoof. The film was *High Anxiety*.

Impressed by his performance in *Silent Movie*, Brooks decided to give himself another starring role as Dr Robert Thorndyke, newly appointed director of the Psycho Neurotic Institute for the Very *Very* Nervous. His predecessor was a victim of foul play and the conspiratorial glances of the matron (Cloris Leachman, doing a variation on Frau Blücher) and head psychiatrist (Harvey Korman) give us a clue as to who might be responsible.

The plot – also involving Madeline Kahn as the daughter of a missing scientist – plays a larger part than usual in a Brooks film, although it is the set pieces you remember: Brooks being pummelled by a bell-boy wielding a rolled-up newspaper in the shower (newsprint rather than blood is seen trickling down the plug-hole); Madeline Kahn being turned on by heavy breathing on the phone, which turns out to be the sound of Brooks being strangled in a phone booth; the camera smashing through french windows in a slow zoom shot of a dinner party – a classic example, incidentally, of the kind of impulsive trickery Brooks is always at pains to disown. It is clear from such tricks that when Brooks (or a well respected member of his repertory) hits on a good idea during filming it invariably finds its way on to the screen, regardless of the wounds it may inflict on the narrative flow.

Brooks, in the role of Dr Thorndyke the archetypal ingenuous fall guy, plays just about as straight as he is able, with the notable exception of one scene in which he renders the title song Sinatra-style, proving in the process that he does indeed have an excellent singing voice. This is one of those occasions when the exhibitionist in Brooks, always straining at the leash, proved irresistible.

The film is dedicated to Alfred Hitchcock and, if anything, Brooks is inclined to err on the side of reverence. Whilst appreciating that he had no wish to offend a living legend, whom he admires enormously, one can't help noticing the tameness of the beast compared to the mad anarchy of *Blazing Saddles* and the stylistic flair of *Young Frankenstein*. Here he seems to have

opted for technical tricks and gags at the expense of atmosphere and tension, vital components in any Hitchcock film, and therefore any spoof. There is nothing in *High Anxiety* to match the superb monster-activating sequence from *Young Frankenstein* in terms of visual excitement, and Dr Thorndyke's fear of heights is never more than a rather ineffective running joke.

Madeline Kahn, as the troubled blonde, every inch a Hitchcock heroine, emerged with honours once again, and Cloris Leachman's sadistic lethal-breasted matron made a worthy addition to her growing gallery of grotesques. But the film did not enjoy the same world-wide success as *Blazing Saddles* and *Young Frankenstein* and the film pundits, noting the missed opportunities, began to speculate about Brooks's future. Had the great movie spoofer burnt himself out? Was it time for a change of direction?

42

Top: Brooks and his two accomplices (Marty Feldman and Dom DeLuise) first encounter Bernadette Peters in Silent Movie.
Bottom: Highly anxious in High Anxiety.

NEXT STOP,

THE WORLD

Throughout his life Mel Brooks has been a firm believer in self improvement, both professionally – since any film director is only as good as his last movie – and privately to make up for his rather inadequate education. He 'discovered' Russian literature in his teens and the vision of writers like Tolstoy and Dostoievsky undoubtedly made a lasting impression on the eager young man. 'I was overwhelmed,' he has said of Tolstoy, 'he writes like an ocean, in huge rolling waves.'

Like most imaginative people Brooks is also fascinated by history, not only because it boasts so many good stories but more importantly 'it teaches us how to survive'. Appropriately, Brooks now turned the pages of history in search of material for a film that would ensure his survival, an epic in the good old Cecil B. DeMille tradition, with a cast of thousands and budget of millions.

When he had finished shooting *High Anxiety*, Brooks was asked 'what next?' by one of the studio hands. 'Something big,' he replied. 'How big?' Mel thought for a moment: 'History of the world!' The more he thought about it the more the idea appealed, though he later modified it to the more manageable *History of the World Part 1*, making a nonsense of the film industry's obsession with sequels. Never for a moment did he intend to make Part 2, despite the mouth-watering trailer at the end of part 1, promising Hitler on Ice and Jews in Space.

Unlike his previous films, *History of the World* could scarcely be described as a genre parody though he regarded it as a tribute to 'the majesty of Cecil B. DeMille, and D. W. Griffith,' the two pioneers of historical epics. 'I used them only in terms of capturing the grand scale of human behaviour stylistically on film. My job as a comedy film-maker is to point out and remind us of what we are – to humble us and expose our foibles.'

To achieve this process of abasement and revelation, he ransacked four historical periods – prehistoric, Roman Empire, Spanish Inquisition and French Revolution – and applied the by now familiar Brooks treatment of streetwise dialogue and sledgehammer wit. In the opening sequence, narrated by Orson Welles, a party of apemen is seen beating their chests, and other parts, with cumulative glee, after which we learn how man invented song – by dropping boulders on the human foot, thereby prompting tuneful squeals of pain.

We move on to the Roman Empire where Comicus, a stand-up philosopher (guess who) is in search of employment. When questioned about the precise nature of his work by the employment officer, Comicus explains: 'I coalesce the vapour of human behaviour into logical comprehension.' 'Oh,' says the dour civil servant, 'a bullshit artist.' Comicus is booked to play Caesar's Palace, the best venue in town, but a disaster if you should displease the Emperor (Dom DeLuise, more than usually gluttonous). In the event, Comicus goes down like a lead balloon – a frantic spoof on the panic which seizes stand-up comedians when they know they're 'dying' on their feet. Desperate for entertainment, Nero orders a fight to the death between Comicus and a black slave, Josephus (Gregory Hines) whom Comicus earlier rescued from a slave auction. They manage to escape, with the help of the Empress Nympho (Madeline Kahn in robust form) and her vestal virgins, and Comicus finds work as a waiter at the Last Supper ('Are you all together or is it separate checks?') Kahn is at her lascivious best in the scene where she selects escorts for the forthcoming orgy from a line-up of de-bagged centurions, like a ravenous vegetarian sizing up the courgettes.

By far the most inventive sequence in *The History of the World* is the Spanish Inquisition, which only Brooks could envisage as a song and dance spectacular of mind-boggling vulgarity. Torquemada (guess who) comes on like Donald O'Connor, grinning from ear to ear and singing merrily about his mission to convert the Jews, whom we see suspended in various forms of bondage throughout the auto-da-fé, including human fruit machines, fetching up three rabbis when fun-loving Torquemada pulls the lever. 'You've flattened their fingers, you've branded their buns, nothing is working so send in the nuns,' sings Torquemada, whereupon a dozen nuns enter, divest their habits to reveal bathing suits and dive in formation into a conveniently placed pool to perform a Busby Berkeley-type routine.

'Too much bad taste!' bellowed Brooks when challenged by one critic. 'There's not enough . . . I love bad taste, I am the spokesman for bad taste. I didn't do it to make fun of the Jews, I did it to make fun of oppression. Comedy brings religious persecutors, dictators and tyrants to their knees faster than any other medium. Poking fun at Torquemada is a wonderful counterpoint to the horrors he committed.'

Similarly Louis XVI, in the ubiquitous person of Mel Brooks, comes in for some savage, if unsubtle satire in the French Revolution sequence. The streets of late 18th century Paris are filled with the starving and the destitute. One street trader touts apple cores from a tray, another dead rats. Times are very hard indeed – and revolution is just around the corner.

At the court of King Louis in the Palace of Versailles (it was actually filmed at Blenheim Palace, England) life is sweet and everyone eats cake at all hours of the day. The King sits on his throne playing outdoor chess with life-size pieces while the people of Paris plot his overthrow at the rat-infested home of Madame Defarge (Cloris Leachman sporting the world's biggest wart). They crave vengeance on a King whose self-indulgence knows no bounds. Bosomy ladies of the court, like the clay pigeon peasants on the shooting range, are fair game for this strutting royal hot-shot, who likes to remind us: 'It's good to be the King,' whilst indulging his divine right.

What plot there is revolves around the King's resemblance to the garçon de pisse (also played by Brooks) who is called upon to double for Louis when the peasants march on Versailles. The double also has to contend with Mademoiselle Rimbaud (Pamela Stephenson), a young lady of impeccable character, who has nevertheless promised her virtue to the King in exchange for her father's freedom.

The sequence reaches its climax at the guillotine where Louis's double is about to get the chop, only to be rescued in the nick of time by . . . Josephus, the Roman slave, in his trusty chariot. You have to go back to *Blazing Saddles*, or the Marx Brothers, to find a crazier ending than that. Indeed there are many other comparisons between the two films, notably the use of current

Who would have guessed the Spanish Inquisition was so much fun?

idioms in an historical context and that un-ashamedly juvenile sense of fun. Practically the first thing Nero does on entering his palatial auditorium is to let fly a fart worthy of applause.

'*History of the World* throws down new challenges to all our notions of taste,' wrote the critic of the London Times. 'If you can detach yourself from your inhibitions, there is a wonderful cathartic and cleansing effect in Brooks's villainies.' David Castell of the Sunday Telegraph found the film 'a blast of real smelly air in a sanitised and deodorised world. While other cinema-bred comics tickle the funny bone, Brooks follows the stand-up tradition of goosing the audience into reaction.'

Brooks may well have been influenced or inspired by the 1969 historical spoof, *Start the Revolution Without Me*, directed by Bud Yorkin, co-written by Fred Freeman and Larry Cohen, and starring Donald Sutherland and Gene Wilder (he made it straight after *The Producers*) in a ludicrous tale of mistaken identity. Like Brooks in his French Revolution bit, Yorkin used British actors like Hugh Griffith, Billie Whitelaw and Victor Spinetti to play the leading French protagonists. The result was a frenetic cosmopolitan ragbag with some inspired moments and spirited performances – in fact a film in the Brooks style.

At one time Brooks was anxious to use the English comedian John Cleese in the Roman Empire sequence, but they both decided it was too much like his appearance in Monty Python's *Life of Brian*, which had been enjoying enormous box office on both sides of the Atlantic. Though no one could accuse *Life of Brian* of taking itself seriously, it seemed an altogether more substantial and acerbic piece of creative lunacy than the Brooks film, despite a considerably lower budget.

Brooks talks of the serious import of his films, bursting the balloon of pomposity and ridiculing oppression, but he is inclined to undermine his own credibility as a film-maker worthy of serious consideration by doubling as the clown.

He plays no fewer than five characters in *History of the World*, each one crazy as a fox,

and expects us to leave the cinema pondering the evils of religious persecution and inherited wealth. It may well be true, of course, that the way to put messages and morals across to a mass audience is by submerging them in a welter of vulgarity, madness and excess. Brooks obviously feels he will reach a far wider and more receptive audience with ridicule and scorn than a solemn documentary spelling out the evils that men do.

Religion and race, the terrible twins, have always tempted and provoked him, partly through his own background and experience, and partly because they do provide a virtually inexhaustible source of comedy material. When it comes to sex, however, Brooks takes a more conventional, not to say old fashioned, line. Not for him the licence assumed by most contemporary film-makers. For a man who is frequently accused of breaking the boundaries of acceptable taste, Brooks is known to be positively prudish with regard to nudity and the portrayal of sex on the screen.

Indeed it is interesting to note that in all his films, except *High Anxiety*, the central relationship is between two men: Bialystock and Bloom in *The Producers*, Vorobyaninov and Bender in *The Twelve Chairs*, Bart and The Waco Kid in *Blazing Saddles*, Frankenstein and Igor in *Young Frankenstein*, Comicus and Josephus in *History of the World*.

Buddy-Buddy partnerships are familiar enough in the cinema, from Laurel and Hardy to Butch Cassidy and the Sundance Kid, but even Brooks is hard put to explain why it should be quite so persistent a feature of his work: 'I'm pretty sure my need to have male characters come together and be close is not some sort of sexual need I've displaced into these people. I think it goes back a lot further than sex, all the way back to my father, whom I never really knew and cannot remember. Maybe in having the male characters in my movies find each other, I'm expressing the longing I feel to find my father and be close to him.'

The women in his films fall into three

cartoon categories. Firstly, the Playboy-type sex object, figment of the male ego, as exemplified by Ula, the gyrating Swedish secretary in *The Producers*, and Miriam, the vestal virgin in *History of the World*. Secondly, the man-eating femme fatale, played almost exclusively by Madeline Kahn. And thirdly, the Amazonian old crone with sadistic, if not actually psychopathic, inclinations, usually played by Cloris Leachman.

These dated stereotypes are, of course, in keeping with the general air of unreality and caricature, but they also represent the director's own view of sex-as-entertainment. Unlike Woody Allen and Neil Simon, Brooks has no interest in taking sex, or even relationships, seriously in his films, because he feels an audience becomes confused if broad comedy suddenly switches to emotional sincerity half-way through a movie. So he prefers to maintain that sense of detachment and surrealism which characterizes his work. Besides, all good Jewish boys are taught at their mother's knee

that sex is something best kept to the privacy of your own room.

The treatment and portrayal of women in his comedies is anachronistic, recalling the Marx Brothers and their treatment of Margaret Dumont and Thelma Todd. They were there either for decoration or as the butt of brotherly fun; rarely, if ever, were they to be taken seriously, let alone treated on equal terms. Though no one would dispute his admiration and fondness for the opposite sex, Mel Brooks treats women in his films with the same jokey, some would say chauvinistic, irreverence. While the strength and intimacy of male friendship (sometimes open to homosexual misinterpretation) has been exploited to full, women have remained strange ornamental intrusions, liable to break your heart (or your neck) if left unattended for any length of time. This explains the antipathy many women feel towards Brooks films.

Apart from Madeline Kahn's gallery of gorgons, the only time Brooks has allowed any real display of female sexuality or

glamour to encroach on this predominantly male domain is in *Silent Movie* when his wife, Anne Bancroft, performs an extravagant tango with the three star finders. Parody it may be, but La Bancroft's natural allure – immortalised in *The Graduate* – makes it as sexy as it is funny. It is the only appearance she has made in one of her husband's movies (discounting *The Elephant Man*, which his company produced) even though she proved herself an accomplished comedienne in *The Prisoner of Second Avenue* with Jack Lemmon. Considering Brooks's tendency to use the same actors in successive movies, Anne Bancroft has been conspicuous by her absence. Her contribution to his success, however, is not to be under estimated.

Mel Brooks makes no secret of the fact that he is Jewish. Indeed he wears it like a badge. His attitude seems to be, to quote Max Bialystock from *The Producers*, 'if you got it, flaunt it.' There is, however, more than a hint of defensiveness in this flamboyant racial pride. In *High Anxiety*, the Hitchcock spoof, Brooks says to Madeline Kahn, as they try to slip through customs disguised as an elderly Jewish couple, 'If you're loud and annoying, people don't notice you.'

A heritage of persecution and despair inevitably colours every facet of Jewish life and consciousness, from the war-torn borders of Palestine to the peaceful verandahs of Los Angeles. For such a beleaguered race, the ability to laugh in the face of adversity has become an essential part of the long-term survival kit.

In an interview with Playboy in 1966, Mel Brooks was asked why so many top comedians and comedy writers were Jewish. His reply said it all: 'When the tall, blonde Teutons have been nipping at your heels for thousands of years, you find it enervating to keep on wailing. So you make jokes. If your enemy is laughing how can he bludgeon you to death?'

Shortly afterwards he made *The Producers* about the staging of a musical called 'Springtime for Hitler', in which the man who exterminated six million Jews is ridiculed with merciless relish. The film became a cult success, enjoyed by millions, but for Brooks it was a benign expression of vengeance. He was using comedy as a means of bringing a tyrannical anti-Semite to his knees, albeit posthumously. Like all the Jewish comedians of his generation – Woody Allen, Danny Kaye, Sid Caesar, Jerry Lewis, Mort Sahl, Lenny Bruce – Brooks grew up in the shadow of the Nazi holocaust. Even though it was 5,000 miles away, a combination of bitterness, guilt and confusion made these second generation immigrants even more determined to prove to themselves and show their resilience than their hardy forebears.

They were mostly the children of Jews from Eastern Europe, who fled to the land of freedom, justice and opportunity – the *goldeneh medina* (golden country) as they called it – at the end of the last century and beginning of this. Used to living under the watchful eye of the state militia, immigrant Jews were understandably dewy-eyed about the utopian dream awaiting them over the seas. They hadn't reckoned on America's own insidious brand of racial prejudice and the economic stringencies to come.

Many immigrants were highly educated and culturally mature but their accomplishments meant little in the New World and they were obliged to take whatever jobs there were, mostly factory and manual work, in the big east coast cities where Jewish ghettoes soon blossomed into whole areas of tenement dwellings, kosher stores and makeshift synagogues. Even the early Jewish settlers from Germany and Spain looked askance at the new arrivals with their black kaftans, funny beards and alien vernacular.

As the Jews prospered and were to some extent assimilated, the once rigid religious discipline was called into question. Traditionally children had always been force-fed the Hebrew texts from an early age and the Rabbis insisted on high levels of academic and religious knowledge. But the second generation, seduced by the trappings of a consumer society, found more spiritual nourishment in the cinema than the synagogue, to the despair of their parents. Why spend an afternoon reading about the prophet Elijah when you could be scared out of your wits by Frankenstein's monster, or serenaded by Al Jolson?

Yet despite this rebellious attitude to Jewish orthodoxy, the young retained respect for their elders and, prompted by a mixture of guilt and parental hectoring, always seemed to shine at school. The old Hebrew ethos of study and application being the pathway to fulfillment is an obligation no self-respecting Jewish child can escape. Those who react against it are labelled *shlemiel* (fool or scapegoat), an increasingly familiar figure in Jewish literature and entertainment.

Humour may not seem obviously compatible with these lofty ideals, but to find the origins of the Jewish-American showbiz tradition you need only look at the old-style itinerant preachers, who travelled from village to village, delivering informal, folksy sermons, larded with funny stories and homespun philosophy. They were the original precursors of satirists like Mort Sahl and Lenny Bruce, though both sides would doubtless be horrified by the comparison. Because of their aloofness from the pains and problems of ordinary folk, these touring preachers came to play a cherished role among the poor and less educated, providing an accessible alternative to the formal Hebrew code of practice.

Theatricality plays a large part, too, in Hebrew ceremony. Even an empty synagogue emits a histrionic aura, and the service itself has a powerful emotional charge, with the cantor intoning all the suffering and despair embodied in the Hebrew texts. Jewish boys have an early taste of the limelight when they undergo *bar mitzvah*, in which you are expected to take on the burdens of adulthood at 13.

But it is language which most vividly characterises and distinguishes Jewish humour from other kinds. More than any other immigrant tongue, Yiddish has infiltrated and invigorated English as spoken in the States, to such an extent that there are many people in America who don't even realise that words like *shmaltz*, *chutzpah* and *mish-mash* are all Yiddish in origin. Few languages better express the psyche and emotions of its people than Yiddish, and the American immigrants have borrowed English words over the years and altered them to suit their own requirements. Terms of abuse proliferate – *shmuck*, *shlump*, *klutz*, *putz* – perhaps because adversaries have always been in plentiful supply.

In his lively lexicon, 'The Joys of Yiddish', Leo Rosten compares it to a street gamin with a natural instinct for survival – 'bright, audacious, mischievous'. Apart from its charm and expressiveness, Yiddish boasts an incredible range of observational nuances and psychological subtleties. Leo Rosten:

> 'It loves the ruminative because it rests on a rueful past; it favours paradox because it knows that only paradox can do justice to the injustice life; it adores irony because the only way the Jews could retain their sanity was to view a dreadful world with sardonic, astringent eyes.'

As far as Jews are concerned, emphasis and feeling are as important as the words you choose, best illustrated in Mr Rosten's book by this classic story. The scene is a huge rally in Red Square, just after Trotsky has been sent into exile. Stalin holds up his arms to quell the clamouring crowd: 'Comrades! A most historic event! A cablegram of congratulations from Trotsky!' The crowd begins to cheer as Stalin reads out the message: 'You were right and I was wrong. You are the true heir of Lenin. I should apologize.'
An explosion of astonishment and triumph fills Red Square. But in the front row, just below the podium, a little old tailor attracts Stalin's attention: 'Such a message, Comrade Stalin! But I think you read it without the right *feeling*!' Whereupon Stalin raised his hand and stilled the throng once more. 'Comrades! Here is a simple worker, a loyal communist who says I haven't read the message from Trotsky with enough feeling. Come, Comrade, you read this historic communication to the people.' So the little tailor climbs up onto the podium, takes the cablegram from Stalin and begins to read: 'You were right and I was *wrong*? *You* are the true heir of Lenin? *I* should apologize????'

At its heart, Yiddish swings between shmaltz and derision. Likewise Jewish humour. The two invariably meet head on in the work of Neil Simon, though Woody Allen and Mel Brooks have eschewed shmaltz as far as possible. Derision is better box office, especially it seems when it is directed at yourself. In cinematic terms it was the Marx Brothers who set the pace for other Jewish humourists. Their tireless creative lunacy and sparkling repartee did wonders to brighten up the gloomy thirties and it is ironic that the heirs to the Marx legacy – Woody Allen in his early films but primarily Mel Brooks – are faced with exactly the same task nearly 50 years on.

Brooks wants the world to laugh and forget its troubles, an ideal as old as the movie business itself. He aspires to social satire in his movies, but his irrepressible sense of fun conspires against the delivery of messages, except in a sublimated way. We know, for instance, that he intended *Blazing Saddles* to ridicule racial prejudice, but how many people leaving the cinema with a head full of gags would give a second thought to the film's serious intentions?

Woody Allen, on the other hand, is more inclined to wear his heart on his sleeve, telling us all about his hang-ups and shortcomings. Apart from the fact that he writes extremely funny gags, Allen is very much a man of his time, a reflection of the insecurities and pretensions of late twentieth century man, whereas Brooks often appears like a hangover from vaudeville, with his quickfire patter and jaunty gait.

Having worked on the same television show together in the fifties, their careers as writer-directors have developed along similar lines, with roughly the same number of box office hits and flops. 'Woody Allen is a genius,' said Brooks in a Playboy interview, 'his films are wonderful. He's poetic, but he's also a critic. I'm not a critic. I can't just zing a few arrows at life as it thunders by. I have to be down on the ground shouting at it, grabbing it by the horns, biting it! Most people are afraid of death, but I really hate it. My humour is a scream and a protest against goodbye. Why do we have to die? I want to cheat death and the way to do that is to make a lot of noise, so that when Death comes he'll say ''that guy's going to be too difficult to take, let's move on to the next.'' '

Allen is equally preoccupied with death, only his deterrent is hard work. Indeed both men are workaholics, often working on more than one major project at a time. The ultimate goal seems to be, as Brooks once put it, to achieve immortality in their own lifetime.

THE CLOWN PRINCE

If Mel Brooks is the current king of the spoofers then Woody Allen is the funnyman who has been dubbed the Clown Prince of cinema. More recently he has been likened to the Prince of Denmark – a joker playing his Hamlet. It is not, though, that Woody Allen takes his comedy any more seriously than Mel Brooks. Rather that he takes *himself* more seriously. And he takes life more seriously. The human comedy isn't always a laughing matter . . . especially, perhaps, when you have spent over 20 years, as Allen has done, in Freudian analysis. Inside every clown there is a tragedian struggling to get out. According to a cover article in Newsweek in 1978, prior to the release of Allen's jokeless movie *Interiors*, he was not only struggling to get out 'but he's just about made it'. They called him 'the funniest neurotic of our time'.

Yet who would have guessed from the directing debuts of Brooks and Allen that Allen would expand and develop his talent in a way that has carried him beyond Brooks? *The Producers* was a much more assured and promising comedy than Allen's erratic, hit-and-miss *Take the Money and Run*, which was described in a 60-word review by Rex Reed in the New York Times (1969) as 'an alleged comedy' filmed in San Francisco 'because, according to Mr Allen, ''it's a nicer place to spend summer than Cleveland''. But obviously not necessarily a better place to make good movies. I've seen funnier ones come out of the American Legion Hall in Baton Rouge, Louisiana.' Eight years later, while Mel Brooks was still receiving three leers for his brand of comedy, Woody Allen was awarded four Oscars for *Annie Hall*, one of the most popular film comedies ever. He was well on his way to becoming a cult figure in the movies.

Before *Annie Hall*, which marked the transition from slapstick to a more gentle comedy of relationships, Woody Allen had been involved as writer, director or actor – sometimes all three at once – in spoofing more genres than anyone else in the movie business – from the futuristic to the historic, from Tolstoy to Sam Spade.

The heroes of his films are neurotic, shy,

High jinks for the accident prone star of Sleeper.

Lynn Redgrave's chastity is besieged by the court jester (Woody Allen) in Everything You Always Wanted to Know About Sex But Were Afraid to Ask.

misunderstood, accident-prone and totally inept at relating to women. 'When it comes to relationships with the opposite sex, I'm the winner of the August Strindberg award,' confesses one of Woody's characters. Another declares: 'I've never had a relationship with a woman that's lasted longer than the one Hitler had with Eva Braun.' We laugh *with* him, not at him. If Mel Brooks' spoofs are irreverent, Allen's are affectionate. His heroes are endearingly vulnerable in the way they reflect our own anxieties and insecurities.

Take the Money and Run (1969), a spoof on crime and prison movies, had Allen playing a lonely misfit, a timid crook called Virgil Starkwell who has the cops laughing all the way to the jailhouse. When he holds-up a butcher he escapes with 113 veal cutlets. When he holds up the local pet store he gets chased down the street by a gorilla. The film tells its story in a style that parodies the American crime documentary – a dramatised

dossier on the criminal's origins with his parents interviewed in a jokeshop disguise of false nose, moustache and glasses. In the prison episode Virgil tries to break out with a gun carved out of soap and blacked with boot polish. Outside it's raining and the gun turns into a froth of soap suds in his hand. On the chain gang where Virgil gets one hot meal a day ('A bowl of steam') he breaks more toes than rocks swinging the heavy hammer.

In *Bananas* (1971), the second film written and directed by Allen, he played Fielding Mellish, a failed lover who gets involved in a banana republic revolution. At first he is a victim, threatened with murder by the corrupt president. By the end he is the hero emerging as the new president in a bearded revolutionist's disguise. 'Everything about the film feels classic – from the title, which is pure Marx Brothers, to Woody Allen's disguise, which is also pure Marx Brothers,' wrote Roger Greenspun in a review reprinted in a chapter on 'Spoofing' contained in the book 'Contemporary Trends'.

Borrowing the title of David Reuben's best-

E-9

selling sex manual, *Everything You Wanted to Know About Sex, But Were Afraid to Ask* (1971), Allen disregarded the contents and mercilessly parodied the solemn sex experts and educationalists. He scripted the film as a series of farcical sketches under such headings as 'Do Aphrodisiacs Work?', 'Are Transvestites Homosexuals?' and so on. 'This film contains every funny idea I've ever had about sex, including several that led to my divorce,' said Allen. In one sketch he played a court jester tampering with the chastity belt of a Queen played by Lynn Redgrave. Another was a take-off of a television panel game, called 'What's my Perversion?' Gene Wilder played a doctor whose patients included a shepherd in love with one of his flock. The final two sketches were the best examples of Allen's inspired anarchy. One, a horror movie spoof, had John Carradine as a mad scientist

experimenting with silicone and letting loose a giant breast to ravage the countryside before Allen traps it in a giant bra. The other featured Allen as a terrified sperm about to be ejaculated into the world by the body's Mission Control. Tony Randall is the operator with Burt Reynolds on the hot line.

In *Play it Again Sam* (1972), which Allen wrote and starred in, he plays Alan Felix, a fall guy who longs to be a tough guy, a fanatical movie buff, haunted by the ghost of Humphrey Bogart. Deserted by his wife he looks up to the Bogart image for advice on romance while his sex life turns into a petrified forest. He scares women away with his small talk, which includes such gems as: 'Your birthday is on the same date as my mother's hysterectomy', or 'I want to have your Child.' You didn't have to be a Humphrey Bogart fan to enjoy *Play it Again Sam*, but it certainly helped.

Gene Wilder can't take his eyes off ewe in Everything You Always Wanted to Know About Sex But Were Afraid to Ask.

Woody Allen disguised as a domestic robot in Sleeper.

Allan Felix finally gets to act out his favourite scene from Casablanca in Play It Again Sam.

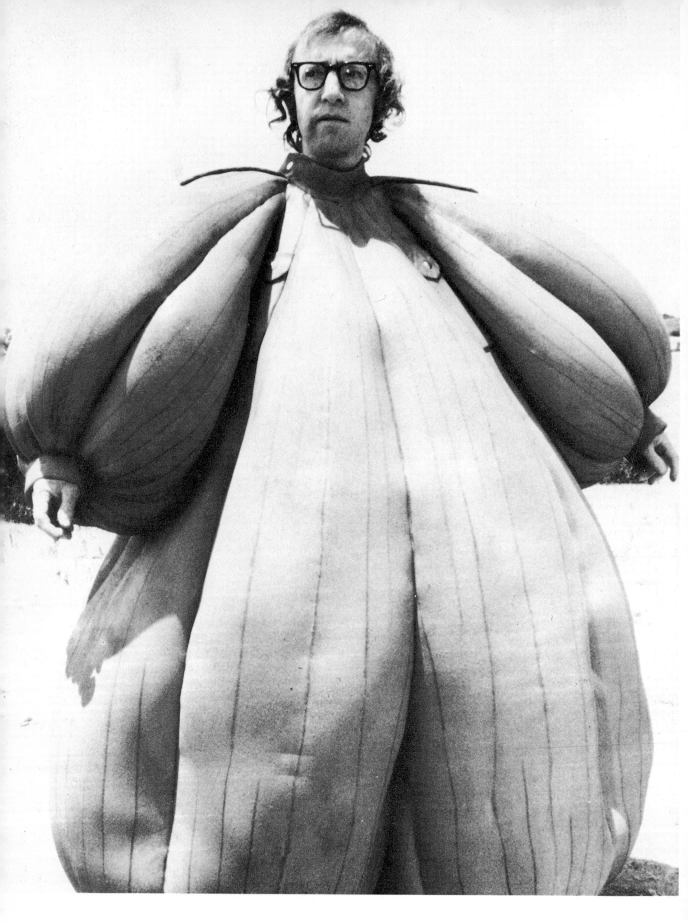

The unacceptable face of inflation in a scene from Sleeper.
Woody finds himself contesting Miss America in Sleeper.

Sleeper (1974), a science fiction spoof, reached a kind of absurd peak (or a peak of the absurd) as a piece of surreal slapstick in which he played Miles Monroe who runs the Happy Carrot health food store until he goes into hospital in 1973 for a routine operation. Complications set in (don't they always in Allen's films?) and he is accidentally and cryogenically frozen until 200 years later when a political underground group defrost him. He wakes up, wrapped in silver foil like a TV dinner, to a kind of 21st century Flash Gordon world. The doctors try to refresh his memory of the old world by showing him pictures (including one of Richard Nixon). 'We think he was a president or something, but we can't find any trace of him.' Later there is a visit to giant fruit where Allen slips on the world's longest banana skin. An ancient Volkswagen car is discovered under a thick layer of cobwebs and starts first time. Allen samples the electronic pleasures of the Orgasmatron machine but decides, after blowing a fuse, 'I don't like things with moving parts unless they're my own.'

Love and Death (1975) was Allen's answer to 'War and Peace' and 'Crime and Punishment'. In an interview in 1981 he picked this film as his personal favourite, perhaps because it combined slapstick with epic parody and pointed satire of sacred cows. *Love and Death* spoofed more cultural targets than any other Allen movie – Bergman, Dostoievsky, Tolstoy, Freud et al. He was spoofing the over-reverence we have for literature and art. He even spoofed the concept of spiritual re-birth. When the Boris/Allen character is executed by Napoleon's firing squad, Sonja (Diane Keaton) asks what it's like to be dead when she sees him being led away by the Grim Reaper: 'It's bad,' he says. 'How bad?' she asks. 'You know the chicken at Treskey's restaurant?' he replies, 'it's worse!' Woody's humour is born out of his (and our) hopelessness. And rarely before has any hero been so hopeless – or so funny.

It's no accident that *Love and Death* as a title contains two of Allen's major preoccupations. Another is God. The fact that Allen is compared with Mel Brooks is, he says, 'inevitable, I suppose, because we're both making funny films at the same time. But I'm much too aware of our differences to be able to see similarities.

'Still, there is no doubt that his pictures make more money than mine, much more money. Why? I think that maybe people feel Mel is kidding, just fooling around with monster movies and cowboy movies, and that it's all quite innocent. But they feel that

when I'm kidding, I'm making fun of God and Mother and human relationships failing, and that bothers them.

'I'm not talking about the big cities . . . there my films do extremely well. But people across the country don't like kidding God and Mother. They like to go to the movies and not be threatened, and non-threatening pictures do the best. Still, I will not play down to an audience for the sake of bigger box-office.'

It was on the Sid Caesar TV show where Allen, then a joke prodigy, just out of his teens, met older writers like Mel Brooks, Larry Gelbart and Danny Simon (Neil's brother). They were people whose funniness was in direct proportion to their anxieties and depressions. According to an interview with Jack Kroll these true manic depressives were very friendly and helpful to Allen. In 1978 Allen and Brooks met again and took a walk on Madison Avenue. 'Is it any better now?' Allen asked Brooks. Did he suffer less? 'We talked about the same things we talked about 20 years ago – ageing, women and death.'

As the 'suffering joker', Woody Allen

admits that making his films is a lot less enjoyable for him than it is for his audiences who watch them. 'It's not much fun. It is hard work and tedious. Mel Brooks has a wonderful time on his movies,' he told David Goodman. 'He loves to make them, they laugh, they have a good time. They hate it when the picture is over. My atmosphere is not like that. It's quiet. It's sullen. The cameraman and the crew get hot-tempered, depressed, dissatisfied . . . it's not a very wonderful atmosphere.'

If truly great comedy must involve something beyond laughter, Woody Allen is certainly in search of it. If plain laughter is a yardstick of good comedy, then Mel Brooks has a long measure of success. Comedy emerges from suffering. The slip on a banana peel is a joke at someone else's painful expense. It has even been seriously suggested by some sources (long before Mel Brooks' *History of the World*) that Stone Age man discovered humour when one caveman dropped a rock on another's head. Woody Allen more than any other joker currently in the movie business personifies the dilemma of a man caught in the serious business of comedy and finding it no laughing matter. 'If you want to make people weep, you must weep yourself. If you want to make people laugh, your face must remain serious,' said Casanova. 'The world is a comedy to those that think, a tragedy to those that feel,' said Horace Walpole. 'I was breast-fed from falsies,' said Woody Allen.

'Look, I have a lot of personal problems and always had,' says Woody. 'But I was lucky in that I had a sense of humour which I could use in my work. It's an important ability for everybody, but particularly for comedians.' People forget that some of the world's funniest men have a tragic side. 'Richard Pryor is a very good comedian, but for a long time he was held up by problems with dope. Lenny Bruce O.D'd and Mort Sahl, who's brilliant, couldn't get along with people. Fortunately I've always had just enough mental health so that I was always able to work and relate to people.'

As Woody's films became more assured and successful so did his heroes. The gap between Virgil Starkwell or Fielding Mellish and Isaac Davies, the hack TV writer in *Manhattan*, or Sandy Bates, the cult movie director in *Stardust Memories* testifies to the development of Allen's character. His films have progressed from visual slapstick to verbal wisecrack. From zany farce to stylish pathos. But the spoof element has always remained. And all that remained to be spoofed by the time Allen arrived at *Stardust Memories* was Allen himself – and his entire dilemma. Time Out called the film Allen's 'first necessary parody'.

Its subject was a cult comedy director who has stopped making funny films and suddenly feels drawn to make serious statements on the human condition. 'He's not funny any more,' was a line in the film spoken to Sandy Bates which was echoed by the critics writing about Allen. Another ungrateful line echoed by the critics was: 'We loved all your films, especially the early comedies.' The trouble with being a comedian is not only that people expect you

to be funny all the time, but they get quite resentful if you stop telling jokes and start being serious.

The worst thing that ever happened to Mel Brooks was being accused of vulgarity, bad taste and lack of discipline. After *Stardust Memories* some sections of the media, like the New York Times, set upon Woody Allen as if, in the words of an impartial London journalist, 'they were setting out to demolish a corrupt president'. 'Woody Allen self-destructs, demolishing his comic persona while parodying and insulting the public that idolises him,' wrote another critic.

But what Allen had done in parodying his fans was no worse that the cinema queue scene in *Annie Hall*, where he overhears a pretentious conversation about Marshall McLuhan and manages to produce the real McLuhan to puncture the pomposity of the conversationalist. True, he went a step further in *Stardust Memories* – he sent up the pseudo intellectuals and elitists who turn art into a religion and prey on culture like vultures. Precisely, in fact, the sort of people who create cult heroes like Woody Allen and then fail to understand them in their hour of need. They just endlessly and thoughtlessly dissect their work as though they were doing an autopsy on a dead man. The greatest killer of comedy is dissection.

The paradox of the funnyman, like Allen, who courts the kiss of death by attempting the profound has been chronicled before by Hollywood in Preston Sturges' 1941 classic *Sullivan's Travels*, in which Joel McCrea played a comedy director who wanted to 'go straight' and make serious 'issue' movies. He eventually discovered that laughter is the best tonic in a world of suffering. 'What have you got to suffer about? Don't you know you have the greatest gift of all – the gift of laughter . . .' the Bates/Allen character is told in *Stardust Memories*. Later he meets a group of super intelligent extra terrestrials and quizzes them about the Meaning of Life. 'You want to do mankind a real service?' they ask. 'Tell funnier jokes.'

Peter Falk flanked by his glamorous co-stars in *The Cheap Detective*. They are in clockwise order, Marsha Mason, Madeline Kahn, Louise Fletcher, Stockard Channing, Eileen Brennan and Ann-Margret.

SPOOFERS IN THE PACK

COPS OR COMICS

Neil Simon is another writer of comedy who walks the tightrope between laughter and tears. He has been a perceptive writer on the human condition; a deadly satirist with a sympathetic touch; a humourist with a heart. He used to be relied upon to provide us with a laughter tonic of slick wisecracks. Lately, with films like the appropriately titled *It Hurts Only When I Laugh* he has added a truthful touch of agony to the bellylaughs.

Like Allen, Simon can't resist a one-line gag in the most extraordinary situations. But while his humour has switched to a new brand of 'concerned comedy' his string of jokes have become necklaces with small pearls of wisdom and perception on subjects like failure, growing old and loneliness. It is precisely because of this depth of perception and quality of caring, shared by Woody Allen and Neil Simon, that they are able to create the highest form of spoofing – the affectionate parody.

It's pure coincidence, one imagines, that they are responsible between them for two of the best spoofs ever made on the tough-guy Bogart image – *Play it Again, Sam* by Allen and *The Cheap Detective* by Simon.

In *The Cheap Detective* Peter Falk, the cross-eyed 'Columbo', played the Chandleresque, Marlowesque, Bogartian detective, Lou Peckinpaugh, who gets involved in four plots in one (*The Big Sleep*, *The Maltese Falcon*, *Casablanca* and *To Have and Have Not*). Despite being a parody, with a plot as thick as the fog that rolled in from San Francisco Bay, the film went out of its way to capture the twilight atmosphere and special look of the forties detective thriller. It had John Alonzo, who shot *Chinatown* and *Farewell My Lovely*, as director of photography. In fact, even as a spoof *The Cheap Detective* displays more feeling for and understanding of the genre it spoofs than did, for instance, Michael Winner's more seriously intended re-make of *The Big Sleep*.

The origins of a lot of the jokes were plain to see for those who knew their Bogart movies. John Houseman, grotesquely padded out, played Jasper Blubber in a send-

Peter Falk talks his way out of a tight spot, with Marsha Mason in The Cheap Detective.

up of Sidney Greenstreet's fat, crooked mastermind of *The Maltese Falcon*.

'How will I recognise you?' asks Peckinpaugh when they arrange to meet in a bar.

'I'll be sitting on two stools by the door,' says the fat man. Peter Lorre's whining, malodorous character, Joel Cairo, from the same movie has become Pepe Damascus, played by the over-sized Dom DeLuise. 'How do you stand being around yourself?' quips Peckinpaugh.

In a take-off of Lauren Bacall's famous scene with Bogie where she asks for a match to light her cigarette, Peckinpaugh is cornered by an alluring creature who invites him to 'Light my fire?' 'I was just looking over your kindling wood,' he replies.

The Cheap Detective was by way of a sequel to another Simon spoof on crime and detection called *Murder by Death*, which parodied the Agatha Christie-style whodunit. This time, Peter Falk played a San Francisco gumshoe called Sam Diamond, one of five world-famous sleuths 'cordially invited to

dinner and a murder' at a fog-shrouded and isolated English-style country manor house. The host, a creepy, eccentric millionaire (Truman Capote, making his acting debut) announces to his guests that when the clock strikes midnight one of the people in the room will be stabbed twelve times in the back with a butcher's knife. One million dollars is offered to the detective who can solve the forthcoming murder. The host doesn't stay for dinner – he prefers to eat out, a commendable decision given the circumstances. His blind butler (Alex Guinness) has secured the weekend services of a deaf and dumb cook.

The other guest gumshoes who were spoofed were Charlie Chan, rechristened Sidney Wang and played by Peter Sellers; Hercule Poirot, Milo Perrier played by James Coco; the Thin Man, David Niven, and Miss Marples, who became Miss Marbles played by Elsa Lanchester.

Simon called the film his first 'freestyle comedy' without a point to make. It was a piece of pure whimsy. Some critics decided

Ring any bells? Peter Falk and company recreate a famous movie moment in The Cheap Detective.

that Simon did not have the brashness and vulgarity of Brooks to make a comfortable genre satirist. Like Woody Allen, Simon has now returned to finding comedy in human relationships. 'I'm obsessed with maturing,' says Simon.

'You mature through relationships with other people . . . you can't do it alone.' But Simon, like Allen, alleviates the growing pains with comedy.

That Simon should choose to spoof two distinct and separate examples of the crime genre offers further proof, if needed, of their attraction to the parodist. For crime, like horror, has proved one of the richest hunting grounds for spoofs.

Ray Stark who produced *The Cheap Detective*, was also behind the Maltese Falcon spoof, *The Black Bird* (1976), starring George Segal as Sam Spade Jnr – the very opposite of his tough, gallant dad. The slouch hat was about all he inherited. In the thirty five years which had lapsed since the original film, even Sam's surname had taken on new shades of meaning, hence the line: 'We don't allow Spades in this hotel!' David Giller's spoof even cast a couple of survivors from the original 1941 movie – Lee Patrick was still secretary to the detective agency with a waiting room of weirdos, including drag artists and flashers) and Elisha Cook Jnr was still the classic fall-guy, seen here falling head-first into a plate of spaghetti. Towards the end, *The Black Bird* flew off into the realms of farce with a midget in a Nazi uniform, Sam Spade in priest's clothing and Lionel Stander as a dim-witted heavy in a frogman's suit doing a spoof on *Jaws*.

From Francis Ford Coppola's Zoetrope Studios (and photographed to look like 'Black Mask' covers) came another pastiche of the Maltese Falcon which, according to one critic, had 'every prop of the American film noir hanging into it except Bogart's trenchcoat'. The film was *Hammett* (1982) and starred Frederic Forest as the pulp-mystery writer Dashiel Hammett in an imaginary adventure in night-time

Alec Guinness as the butler who might have done it, is grilled by Peter Falk in Murder by Death.

Chinatown with his own fictional detective. Set in the 1920s it merged life and art in a touching way.

In Mike Hodges *Pulp* (1972), Michael Caine played another thriller-writer who finds fiction turning uncomfortably into fact. When he gets a crooked commission to ghost-write the biography of an ex-Hollywood movie star and mobster, played by Mickey Rooney, he finds that pulp means pulverised bodies, as well as cheap paperback novels. Gun blasts and corpses no longer vanish at the turn of a page or the end of a chapter. The film featured a cop who was a reincarnation of Bogart and a moth-eaten bird on a perch referred to as the Maltese Falcon. The film was actually shot in Malta.

Apart from Hammett and *The Maltese Falcon*, Raymond Chandler's detective Philip Marlowe has been spoofed with affection or irreverence more than any other sleuth.

Indeed Humphrey Bogart himself sent up the crime melodrama which made him so famous in John Huston's 1954 film, *Beat the Devil*, scripted by Truman Capote and co-starring Peter Lorre from *Casablanca* and *The Maltese Falcon*. The Herald Tribune in New York called the film 'a burlesque of all movie melodramas.

Bogart didn't share the joke. He thought that only phony intellectuals thought it was funny. It seems that Bogart didn't realise that Huston had used him as a straight man to set off chain reactions among the comedians. He thought the film had been ruined. It is now regarded as a brilliant satire with a cult following. Critic Pauline Kael puts it in the 'fluke-classic' category which only goes to demonstrate that spoofs can be accidental as well as intentional.

In the British spoof *Gumshoe* (1971), Albert Finney played Eddie Ginley, a Bingo caller in a Liverpool working men's club who dreams like Woody Allen's Alan Felix of being a

Peter Falk with the man of a thousand faces, Peter Sellers, spoofing Charlie Chan, in Murder by Death.

Bogart tough-guy. On his thirty first birthday he puts a private-eye advertisement in his local paper as a joke. But his services are called upon for real by a mysterious fat man – looking like a corrupt cousin of Sidney Greenstreet. The plot led us through all the hallmarks of the forties thriller, with the wisecracks and throwaway lines.

In *Shamus* (1972), starring Burt Reynolds, there were a couple of scenes which were obvious pastiches on *The Big Sleep*. In one, Reynold's private-eye is hired by an eccentric millionaire who suffers a medical condition that requires him to sit in a refrigerated room instead of a hothouse. Reynolds shivered where Bogie sweated. The other scene is in a bookshop where Reynolds carries Bogie's gallant pass at a lady to the less subtle limits allowed by the permissive cinema of the seventies.

Jack Smight's *Harper* (1966) (re-titled *The Moving Target* in Britain) starred Paul Newman in another pastiche of *The Big Sleep*. Lauren Bacall appears in an in-joke, not in her old role but as a rich bitch confined to a wheelchair, who hires an insolent private-eye (Newman) to find her missing husband. Smight's film was a big hit and was responsible for a spate of spoofs on the private-eye theme that followed. Frank Sinatra played a slickly entertaining private-

eye in *Tony Rome* (1967) and *The Lady in Cement* (1968) and James Garner was a lightweight *Marlowe* in the 1969 film directed by Paul Bogart and featuring a spoof on a karate killer who demolished Garner's office with bare hands – and feet. The story was taken from Chandler's 'The Little Sister' and provided the usual private-eyeful of corpses and earful of wisecracks.

Art Carney was an ageing one-time private-eye in Robert Benton's *The Late Show* (1977) in which Lily Tomlin played an eccentric who hires him to find her missing cat. If spoof can be counted as a nostalgic recreation of a durable genre then Dick Richards' re-make of *Farewell My Lovely* starring Robert Mitchum qualifies, too. David Zelag Goodman's script preserved some of Chandler's own memorable wisecracks, e.g. 'She gave me a smile I could feel in my hip pocket.' Mitchum again played Marlowe in Michael Winner's re-make of *The Big Sleep* which transplanted the action for some reason from Chandler's corrupt California to cosy England.

Richard Dreyfuss played Moses Wine, ladies' man, private-eye, ex-student radical and ex-husband in *The Big Fix* (1978), based on Roger L. Simon's book, which showed 'The Big Sleep' reawakened in a California of the 1970s. One day Wine is minding other

*Gene Wilder and Madeline Kahn in The Adventures of
Sherlock Holmes' Smarter Brother.*

Marty Feldman presents Gene Wilder with a vital clue – or is it a parking ticket? – in The Adventures of Sherlock Holmes's Smarter Brother.

people's business for a living. The next he is a special investigator for a presidential candidate discovering that what seemed to be nothing but a smear campaign from the opposition is a front for extortion, devil worship, sex orgies and murder.

In John G. Avildsen's private-eye parody Super Dick (1971) Allen Garfield was an over-weight indiscriminately amorous detective who found all clues leading to sexual perversion.

Robert Altman cast Elliott Gould as Philip Marlowe in The Long Goodbye as a 1973 version of the detective who was still driving a 1948 Lincoln Continental and trying to behave like Bogart . . . unsuccessfully. Harrassed by the cops at the precinct station he wiped finger print ink on his face and broke into an imitation of Al Jolson. According to Pauline Kael The Long Goodbye to the private-eye hero is 'less accidental than Beat the Devil though quicker-witted . . . it reaches a satirical dead-end that kisses off the private-eye form as gracefully as Beat the Devil finished off the cycle of the interna-

tional intrigue thriller.'

Far from accidental was Never a Dull Moment (1967) in which Edward G. Robinson parodied a type he once played so earnestly by playing a mobster called Joe Smooth whose henchmen 'kidnap' a TV gangster actor (Dick Van Dyke) whom they mistake for a real villain.

Leaving aside the private-eye and gangster movie which has inspired so many followers brings us to the Wilder and Wilder exploits of Sherlock Holmes: first Billy Wilder's The Private Life of Sherlock Holmes (1970) and then Gene Wilder's The Adventures of Sherlock Holmes Smarter Brother (1975).

These spoofs on the great sleuth were quite different. Billy Wilder's film was an affectionate pastiche that retained respect without being too reverent. Together with co-writer I.A.L. Diamond – who is to Wilder what Watson was to Holmes – a mystery was created which involved a Loch Ness 'monster', midgets with ancient faces, Trappist monks and dead canaries. The

relationship between Holmes (Robert Stephens) and Watson (Colin Blakely) is treated with humour throughout the film. Was Holmes a homosexual? Messrs Wilder and Diamond safely restored his reputation (after some camp cavorting) with Holmes' encounter with a Belgian beauty (Genevieve Page) who sleep-walks naked through his apartment and offers him a clue where you would least expect it. Earlier in the film there is an outing to the ballet where Watson is caught indulging in some camp choreography at a backstage party. The whole of this Swan Lake episode was done in the style of Wilder's most outrageous hit *Some Like it Hot*.

Gene Wilder's film was calculated to give Sir Arthur Conan Doyle a nastier turn in his grave, since it has little to do with the original. As well as directing, Gene Wilder played the eponymous 'Smarter Brother' who unkindly refers to his older brother's exploits by deriding him as 'sheer luck' Holmes. Three other stars from the Mel Brooks' school of comedy joined in the send-up – Madeline Kahn as a music hall singer who is being blackmailed; Marty Feldman as the bungling Scotland Yard assistant; and Dom DeLuise as the blackmailing opera singer. Any film that invents a smarter (in truth, dumber) brother for Sherlock Holmes has to be saluted as inventive at the very least. As the jealous, younger brother to whom Sherlock delegates the 'Bessie Bellwood blackmail case', Sigerson Holmes – Sigi to his friends – falls in love. Wilder created a velvet, Victorian atmosphere in his film with brass oil lamps, hansom cabs and London fog. Sherlock Holmes and Dr Watson were played by veteran British actors Douglas Wilmer and Thorley Walters.

Dom Deluise also made his directing debut, like Wilder and Allen, with a crime spoof, called *Hot Stuff*. This was a whimsical account of a real-life operation in which DeLuise and a team of plain clothes cops decide to boost their conviction rate by taking over a fencing operation to ensnare crooks. The array of comedy character actors who paraded through the film were described by one critic as the most colourful felons outside of Damon Runyon's stories.

Other comic cops who have maintained law and disorder on the screen are *Freebie and the Bean*, alias James Caan and Alan Arkin, who under the direction of Richard Rush in 1974 found themselves involved in a mixed bag of slapstick stunts and icy, blood-spilling showdowns. Some of the stunts had little to do with the story but were nevertheless marvellous – like Caan's timid request for a tow truck to be sent to the third floor (sic) of the apartment building his squad car has just wrecked.

Like *Freebie and the Bean*, *Fuzz* (1972) was a film that mixed spoof humour with sick homicide in a tale about a rookie bunch of cops trying to catch the bad guys. Raquel Welch played a detective who in turn played a well-endowed decoy on a rape case and Burt Reynolds and Jack Weston disguised themselves as nuns.

There is no end, it seems, to the ingenuity of the spoof. In Alan Parker's gentle parody of the 1930s Hollywood gangster film, *Bugsy Malone* (1976) he used children to play the rival gangsters and avoided blood and bullets by loading their 'splurge' guns with nothing more deadly than a concoction of custard cream. Meanwhile, the film parodies a whole inventory of cinema cliches, from a barber's shop ambush to newspaper headlines flashing across the screen to spread word of the gang's exploits.

If the James Bond films contained elements of self-parody without actually spilling over into 'pure' spoof they did prompt a craze in the 1960s for spoof spy films in which the jokes took over from the storyline. In these usually mindless and sexist send-ups of kissing and killing the push-button, gadget-ridden secret agent arrived at overkill. Watches did everything but tell the time and in one film a cigarette lighter featured 82 uses – 83 if you actually lit a cigarette with it. There was drugged lipstick, cigarettes with laughing gas, flame-throwing fountain pens, expendable blondes and exotic locations.

Dean Martin was secret agent Matt Helm in

BM.1551

a series of films – *The Ambushers*, *Murderers Row*, *The Silencers* and *The Wrecking Crew*. James Coburn was *Our Man Flint* – another chip off the Bond block – and *In Like Flint*. *Casino Royale*, which arrived about five years after 'Dr. No', the first Bond film, was a slapstick extravaganza that features six James Bonds (including Woody Allen as little Jimmy Bond and David Niven as Sir James Bond, retired) under the corporate camerawork of five directors (including John Huston and Ken Hughes). In 1966 Joseph Losey came up with 'the James Bond film to end all James Bond films'. It was called *Modesty Blaise* and it looked as if it had been shot through a kaleidoscope instead of a camera. Even bombs exploded in twirling clouds of blue and green smoke. The film was advertised as the female James Bond under the slogan 'Deadlier than the Male' – which, in the never ending proliferation of spy spoofs, became the title for yet another. Based on the popular newspaper comic strip, the film starred Dirk bogarde, Monica Vitti and Terence Stamp.

Ingenuity was never at a loss during the spy boom send-up. There was even a canine contender in the British film *The Spy With a Cold Nose*. It was enough, at times, to make the most ardent fan want to defect.

In 1974 Elliott Gould and Donald Sutherland teamed up again to do for the CIA what they did for Army combat surgeons in *M.A.S.H.* The film was, predictably called *S.P.Y.S* but as a pair of bungling secret agents involved in, among other things, an exploding Paris pissoir, they failed to repeat the success of Altman's film in this new context.

Blake Edwards' Pink Panther films did, however, get a new lease of life 13-years after the first film appeared when, in 1976, Edwards embarked on more obvious send-ups. *The Pink Panther Strikes Again* was a James Bond spoof in which Inspector Dreyfus held the world to ransom with his Doomsday Machine to revenge himself against Clouseau. Two years later *The Revenge of the Pink Panther* sent up *The Godfather*. These two films subsequently appeared along with Mel Brooks' parodies and other spoofs (*Kentucky Fried Movie*) on Variety magazine's listings of the most successful comedies in Hollywood history.

The last true espionage spoof spied upon by us was Clive Donner's *The Nude Bomb* (1980), which featured Sylvia (*Emannuelle*) Kristel in a secret agent burlesque based on the American television comedy series, 'Get Smart'. Don Adams repeated his role as the accident-prone, Clouseau-like agent, with Rhonda Fleming and Vittorio Gassman completing the cast. Clive Donner, of course, is no stranger to the art of spoof after directing *Luv, Vampira* and *What's New, Pussycat.*

On the whole it can be said that the spy spoofs left their audiences feeling like the Bond martini – shaken but not stirred.

LAUGH, I NEARLY DIED

The inspired inanities and endless variations of the spoof film can be truly impressive. Just as the crooks, cops, private-eyes and spies prove arresting material for the parodist, so do vampires, werewolves and other monster movies. A sense of horror, like a sense of humour, is strictly personal. One man's groan can so easily be another's guffaw. The line between the ludicrous and the horrific is thin, like the line between comedy and tragedy, and requires a delicate sense of balance or, in some cases, an unbalanced mind. If you don't always laugh because maybe you can't see the joke, perhaps you laugh just to relieve the tension.

Hitchcock's *Psycho*, now universally acclaimed as a classic horror, was greeted with a similar mixture of outrage and laughter when it opened in Britain in 1960. 'Hitch, old cock . . . this is the worst film you have made,' wrote one critic. 'Scenes inspiring the wrong kind of laughter,' wrote The Times critic. Sometimes even when you're trying to be serious (though Hitchcock did have a black sense of humour) you can be accused of playing a joke. Or was Hitchcock, after all, one of the great spoofers? He is said

to have been perturbed that audiences took *Psycho* seriously. But when *do* we take Hitchcock seriuslty? When he wanted to show just how difficult it is to kill a man, the resulting scene in *Torn Curtain*, with Paul Newman, was received by laughter. No wonder Mel Brooks was drawn to make *High Anxiety*.

Sometimes we are simply not sure when we are being frightened or humoured. The cinema of menace is full of unintentional (or is it?) mirth – from the killer bees of *Swarm*, who merely stung audiences for the price of admission, to the hopping horror of *Frogs*, the hissing *Ssssnake* and the snapping mini-jaws of *Piranha*. In the horror film, like cop and spy movies, there is a code of conduct, a tradition or ritual which is easily recognised and therefore easily satirised or spoofed. Within the genre conventions, particularly the stereotypes of Dracula and vampire movies, a rich vein has been punctured as spoof movie-makers have injected new blood – not always of the right group.

Roman Polanski made the Dracula send-up *The Fearless Vampire Killers* (1967 *Dance of the Vampires* – GB) after *Repulsion* and before *Rosemary's Baby*. As a spoof, most of it could have been lifted intact from any Hammer horror. At most it was an engaging oddity. For the most of its length there was no horror, and little suspense. Sharon Tate appeared in a bizarre blood-sucking sequence in her bath and a homosexual vampire assaulted Polanski himself, who played a nutty professor's assistant abroad in Transylvania. The best scene was a midnight ball of vampires where the gate crashers were the only figures reflected in a big mirror. (Vampires, of course, show no reflection).

Clive Donner's *Vampira* (1974) featured David Niven as the Count, plus four finalists in a Playboy magazine competition to find the most 'biteable' playmate on the month. The comedy was somewhat coagulated. *Vampyres*, a 1974 British-made film directed by David Larraz, featured lesbian vampires, while the 1972 *Blacula* directed by William Crain, had a black bloodsucker. William Marshall played an African prince who

In later years, Alfred Hitchcock found it difficult to take his reputation seriously.

Roman Polanski gets to the heart of the problem in his spoof, Dance of the Vampires.

arrived in Transylvania to enlist the Count's aid in a crusade to stop the slave trade. Unfortunately he himself becomes a victim of vampirism and is christened Blacula by the Count and imprisoned in a coffin. After 150 years, Dracula's castle is ransacked by two gay antique dealers who become Blacula's first victims as they are shipping his body back to Los Angeles. In California the tale turned into something resembling *Shaft* by Bram Stoker.

Nocturna directed by Harry Tampa in 1978, was described as the first soft-porn-vampire-disco-rock movie — a dubious distinction. The cast included Yvonne de Carlo as Jugulia and John Carradine as Dracula, minus fangs and deploring through his false teeth the lack of good quality blood. Nai Bonet, the executive producer, played Dracula's granddaughter living in the Transylvania castle which had been converted into an hotel to meet taxes. When an American rock group comes to stay she falls in love with one of the musicians and elopes to New York, spending her time between discos and a hideout under Brooklyn bridge.

Nineteen-seventy-nine was a vintage year for bloodsuckers with *Love at First Bite* and *Dracula Sucks*. The latter, directed by Philip Marshak was a sexploitation romp, reported to be hard core in origin, but reduced by the censor's cuts to a rather amateurish shambles. Between the blood-sucking and coitus interruptus the story line followed the fate of a young man taken to a sanatorium where the patients included an Adolf Hitler, a Baby Jane and a Singing Cowboy — all apparently inflicted with sexual hysteria. In the end at least one soul is saved as the doctor lets sunlight fall on the copulating bodies of Dracula and his victim in his coffin.

Stan Dragoti's *Love at First Bite* featured suave George Hamilton as Count Vladimir Dracula, faced with emigrating or sharing an apartment when a People's Commissar announces the annexation of his Transylvania castle as a gymnasium. The Count opts for New York, having fallen in love with a magazine cover girl (Susan Saint James). His manservant arranges a meeting

Dracula (George Hamilton) with a likely lass in Love at First Bite.

with the girl and helps Dracula rob a blood bank when it becomes apparent that New Yorkers hardly blink an eyelid at his batty nocturnal appearances. The romantically tortured Count at last finds the ecstasy of love in bed with Cindy, his cover girl, responding: 'Oh, that's so kinky! Are *you* biting *me*?' Richard Benjamin played Cindy's psychiatrist-boyfriend who has his own neuroses and immediately recognises the puncture marks on Cindy's neck. Mixing up his monsters, he tries to destroy the Count with silver bullets in a restaurant. Noted one critic: 'Much of the film subsequently follows the path trodden by the Mel Brooks' parodies, gleefully subjecting the genre to the same absurd incongrueties but less often departing from it in a quest for laughs at any price.' The gentle send-up worked even better because Hamilton was utterly straight-faced. It was designed as a thirties romantic comedy in which true love conquered all and made its mark because the ludicrous love story was played absolutely deadpan.

Brian De Palma's spoof, *Phantom of the*

Renfield, the cockroach-eating manservant (Arte Johnson) with his master in Love at First Bite.

Paradise (1974), took its cue from the old horror classic *Phantom of the Opera*, and replaced the Lon Chaney character with a long-haired rock music composer who had been accidently disfigured in a record-

John Carpenter's Halloween contained a strong element of spoof.

Frank N. Furter (Tim Curry) on the rampage in The Rocky Horror Picture show.

David Naughton cries wolf with some conviction in An American Werewolf in London

pressing machine trying to recover a stolen pop cantata. The music has been taken by a young impresario for the opening concert at his Paradise Theatre where the masked monster now awaits his revenge.

Another rich musical genius horribly disfigured, this time in a car crash, and planning revenge, was *The Abominable Dr Phibes*, directed in Britain in 1971 by Robert Fuest and starring Vincent Price in his 100th film. Phibes was a horror pastiche done with much panache. The revenge on the surgical team who failed to save his wife's life after the car crash is based on the Old Testament curses of the Pharoah, with visitations of bees, boils and bats, to name just three. Due to his disfigurement Phibes drinks and eats through his right earlobe, or somewhere thereabouts. He can only talk by plugging himself into an old fashioned gramophone horn which makes His Master's Voice sound very scratchy. The spoof was so successful that a sequel, *Dr Phibes Rises Again* (1977), soon followed. This time one of the doctor's victims is washed up on a beach in a giant, corked gin bottle. 'Was he a heavy drinker?' inquired the Scotland Yard detective.

Theatre of Blood (1973) had Price taking a bizarre form of multiple revenge yet again – this time as a Shakespearian actor getting his own back on the eight members of the Critics' Circle who fail to award him their 'Oscar' as actor of the year. Each critic is dispatched to his death in a gruesome parody of the murders in Shakespeare's plays; ie one is dragged through the streets by horses ('Troilus and Cressida'), another is drowned in a barrel of wine ('Richard II'). The Merchant of Menace extracts much more than his pound of flesh.

A futuristic Frankenstein featured in Paul Bartel's 1975 film *Death Race 2000*. Played by David Carradine, he was a mysterious masked competitor in a transcontinental death race across America in which racers competed for not only the fastest time but the highest tally of accident victims. Like Phibes and the Phantom of the Paradise, the mask concealed a body which had reputedly undergone major reconstruction work after a

series of accidents. Other competitors in the race were Sylvester Stallone as Machine Gun Joe Viterbo and Mary Woronov as Calamity Jane. There were reportedly disagreements on the film over the exact proportions of comedy and thick-ear exploitation the film was to contain . . . an example of black comedy was the featured Euthanasia Day at a geriatric hospital when staff wheeled the patients out into the paths of oncoming cars, only to find themselves knocked down like ninepins as Frankenstein swerves to avoid the wheelchair victims.

Another unusual Frankenstein was featured in Jim Sharman's film version of the stage musical *The Rocky Horror Picture Show* (1975), with Tim Curry in black suspender belt and stockings presiding over a plot which included Dracula and references to King Kong and Dr Strangelove. (Sharman directed another spoof musical in 1981 called *Shock Treatment*, which lampooned our love affair with television. It was set in a mythical suburban community so dominated by TV that life itself had become one big TV show, complete with commercial breaks.)

Apart from Dracula and Frankenstein, the other great and gruesome man-made movie monster is the werewolf or wolfman, which prompted one of the most brilliant horror spoofs of recent times, *An American Werewolf in London* (1981). It was genuinely terrifying and, at times, undeniably hilarious. 'I came up with the idea of a werewolf,' said director John Landis, 'because vampires had been done to death (no pun intended) and the werewolf is the only international beast . . . .' The film achieved its aims because it didn't allow the sense of humour to detract from the combination of classic horror and modern shock. One of the great things about successful spoof horror movies is that they really capture the mood of the genre. Hitchcock proved that the tongue in cheek did not stilt moments of tension, and the same is true of horror. Best about the Landis movie were the magnificent special effects – notably the ghastly metamorphosis from human being to howling lycanthrope, and the scene where a London Bobby is

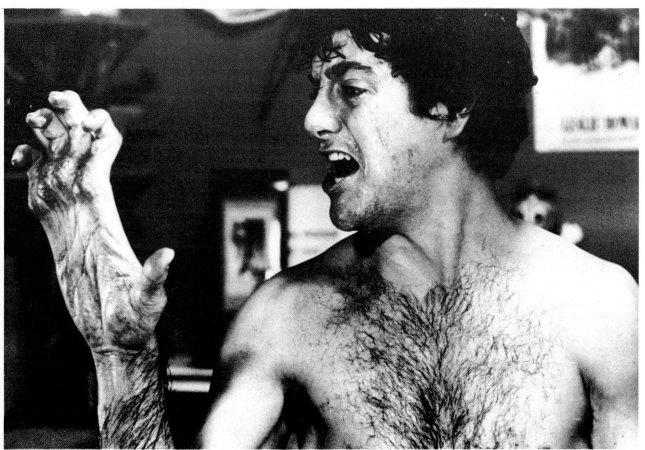

confronted the beast and loses his head, in a manner of speaking. David Naughton looked suitably aghast and perplexed by his changing fortunes as the werewolf and Jenny Agutter played the nurse falling in love with her patient. Landis actually wrote the screenplay for *An American Werewolf . . .* in 1969 but it took eleven years to get it produced 'mainly because it's a genuinely weird picture . . . I really don't think people are prepared for the movie that I'm going to give them,' Landis wrote before it was shown.

In 1973 *The Werewolf of Washington* was conceived as a politico-horror spoof which parodied the werewolf film via a case of Watergate lycanthropy. Dean Stockwell played a rising star of the Washington Press Corps who is attacked by a wolf in the Carpathian mountains and unwittingly brings his affliction to the White House. His early victims included an influential lady publisher and a politically ambitious wife (reportedly not unlike Martha the Mouth). Eventually a silver bullet from the gun of the president's daughter, a former flame, puts an end to his rampage. Writer-director Milton Moses Ginsberg created a topical, as well as an elegant, satire.

A parody of a mythical monster was created by the British Monty Python team member Terry Gilliam with *Jabberwocky*, in 1977. The slimy and fearful monster stalked through medieval forests reducing peasants to smoking skeletons before being slayed in a series of well-timed accidents. Like other send-ups, the film caught the look of its period and the atmosphere more success-fully than many seriously-intentioned competitors.

Veteran American director William Beaudine transported the movie monsters out West in the 1960s when he directed *Jesse James Meets Frankenstein's Daughter* and *Billy the Kid Vs. Dracula*. The former film established Maria and Rudolph Frankenstein – grandchildren of the notorious Baron – in a Mexican village after fleeing from Vienna. Maria is still attempting to transplant artificial brains created by her grandfather when Jesse James turns up, en-route to join the Wild Bunch down south.

In *Billy the Kid Vs. Dracula* (1965), Chuck Courtney played Billy Kid and John Carradine once again played a fangless Dracula (as he did later in *Nocturna*). In one sequence, Dracula vampirises a squaw and, in revenge, the Indians attack a stagecoach and massacre the passengers.

CAUGHT IS THE CROSSFIRE

Over a decade before Mel Brooks struck it rich out West with *Blazing Saddles*, an unknown director Elliot Silverstein made an overnight reputation with his burlesque Western, *Cat Ballou*, in which Lee Marvin played an ageing, whiskey-soaked and apparently washed-up gunslinger. Jane Fonda co-starred as Catherine Ballou, a prim, innocent school-teacher who turns outlaw when her father is shot. '*Cat Ballou* isn't a parody,' wrote Pauline Kael, reviewing the film in 1965, 'that would mean stylizing the conventions of the genre, not just using them and making jokes about them. It's a spoof, and it spoofs the only safe target – itself.' It began a posse of Western spoofs.

Lee Marvin starred in another slapstick Western, *The Great Scout and Cathouse Thursday* (1976), directed by Don Taylor. Sexual innuendo, as well as satire featured in the film's wayward sense of humour. Marvin played a legendary Indian scout with Oliver Reed as a racially prejudiced half-breed who caught a dose of the white man's disease and plans to start an epidemic.

In John Huston's *The Life and Times of Judge Roy Bean* (1972), Stacy Keach did a take-off of Marvin's gunslinger in *Cat Ballou*. He played an albino baddie called Bad Bob who wore black leather to offset his flowing platinum blonde hair. Paul Newman played alongside a grizzly bear co-star as the roguish outlaw who proclaims himself judge and vows to bring peace to a small Texas town, adding '. . .and I don't care who I have to kill to get it.' 'Maybe this isn't the West the way it was,' said Huston. 'But it's the way it should have been!'

Burt Kennedy made a couple of spoof

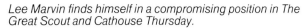
Westerns with James Garner quietly sending up his years in the Maverick role in *Support Your Local Sheriff* (1969) and *Support Your Local Gunfighter* (1971). In the first film he played a sheriff who stops a gunfight by sticking his finger up someone's gun barrel. The second film continued the satirical digs at Western myths, from amiable jokes on fumbled gunplay ('I'm slow, but you're slower') to grisly black humour (after crushing a local tough's right hand, Garner discovers he wears his gun on the left side). Critic Rex Reed wrote of the first film: 'A cracker barrel of marvellous character actors invest this lusty, roaring, brawling spoof of old shoot-em-ups with more charm than mayhem. Without the use of gags or one-liners or flashy camera gimmicks, Burt Kennedy had produced a really delightful movie in which the comedy comes from within the character portraits instead of pies in the face.'

Andrew McLaglen is a director who for many years made Westerns after the style of John Ford, with a strong element of the sentimental. Films like *Shenandoah* (1965) and *The Rare Breed* (1966) were unkindly described as 'slapdash imitations' of Ford in which a certain touch of parody had been overlooked. But with *Something Big* (1971) McLaglen got together an Anglo-American cast (Dean Martin, Brian Keith, Honor Blackman and Carol White) for a film in which the parody was deliberate and unmistakeable. It was something close to the crazy comedies of Howard Hawks. Brian Keith played an ageing cavalry colonel who was about to be retired from his post. The reference to John Wayne's portrayal of Captain Nathan Brittles in Ford's classic *She Wore a Yellow Ribbon* could not be missed.

Melvin Frank's comedy Western, *The Duchess and the Dirtwater Fox* (1976) satirised a profusion of Western stereotypes, with a faithful horse who continually forgets his cues, a whore posing as a Duchess (Goldie Hawn) and a bungling gambler (George Segal).

Under his own direction, Sidney Poitier starred alongside Harry Belafonte in the 1971 Western *Buck and the Preacher*. This was more in the category of a novelty Western than a pure spoof, with Belafonte almost unrecognisable in his caricature of the preacher. But there was a spoof sequence in which the Indians, instead of the cavalry, ride to rescue when all seems lost.

In Howard Zieff's *Hearts of the West* (1975, Hollywood Cowboy–GB) Jeff Bridges mouthed cowboy clichés playing a Western film extra in the 1930s who is also an aspiring screenplay writer involved in fake and real show-downs. The film poked lighthearted fun at Western traditions.

Andy Warhol's 1968 film *Lonesome Cowboys* was variously described as spoof western, weirdo western and circus side-show of fag-hags and homosexuals. Wrote Rex Reed: 'The "cowboys" look like Hollywood Boulevard drag queens who just looted Teepee Town. They get stoned on pot, talk about getting their hair done and ride around on worn-out nags on their last legs before the glue factory.' Others, taking the film more seriously, talked of it as an improvised satire on a theme – ie 'the demythification of the West'. It did, however, have its amusing moments. A cowboy, after pausing to give a trailhand some hints on coiffure, proceeds to practise his ballet exercises on the tethering bar so his thighs will hold six-guns better. 'It'll build up the buns!' he says.

Still caught in a crossfire of flying lead and laughter, we move from the Wild West shoot-up to the battle theatres of the World. Of these, Robert Altman's *M*A*S*H* (1970) was variously labelled outrageous, zany, riotous and insane. Because of its prankishness the film was

regarded by some as a spoof more than a satire. The title was an abbreviation of Mobile Army Surgical Hospital and the comedy followed the antics of a couple of combat surgeons (Donald Sutherland and Elliot Gould) operating three miles from the Korean battlefront. Everyone was a little touched by madness. Nurses were seen stitching the commander's shirts instead of the wounded. The blood bank was full of chilled beer. The helicopter landing strip for emergency wounded is used as a golf course; Gould and Sutherland operate at one point in golf shoes and Japanese kimonos. Meanwhile, the dental officer, who fears he is a latent homosexual, has a Last Supper suicide party and the padre blesses jeeps to deliver from danger those who ride in them.

In Richard Lester's feeble British war spoof, How I Won the War (1967), Michael Hordern shoots a crippled tank to 'put it out of its misery'. While Lester's film contained less pointed slapstick farce, M*A*S*H was an unstoppable haemorrhage of sick humour which made even the bloodless but savage British satire, Oh! What a Lovely War, look tame by comparison.

M*A*S*H marked a watershed in American movie comedy and there were plenty of immitators. Ted Post's C.A.S.H (1975, Whiffs in America) re-cast Elliot Gould as an Army private discharged with a disability pension after working as a guinea pig, testing the products of the chemical corps. The British title stood for 'Chemical Air-Spray Hold-up'. Unable to hold-down a job and suffering impotence, loss of hair and tastebuds, Gould resorts to committing robbery by using laughing gas.

Less of a bellylaugh than an expensive 30million dollar bellyflop was Steven Spielberg's comedy of errors on a grand and ridiculous scale, 1941 (1979). It's difficult to say who spoofed what in this film. Perhaps the joke was really on Hollywood, for giving Spielberg so much money in return for so little entertainment. The 'outrageous story of paranoia, disaster and craziness on a monumental scale' takes place six days after Pearl Harbour when a Japanese submarine surfaces off the coast of California. Its mission – to capture Hollywood. Spielberg spoofed his own film Jaws when a terrified naked girl swimmer finds herself stalked by a submarine instead of a shark.

1941 was a self-indulgent spoof in the style of Hollywood's other epic examples of lunacy – from *Hellzapoppin*, to *It's a Mad, Mad, Mad, Mad World*. It was also, reputedly, the most expensive comedy ever made.

Like many spoof films, *1941* was cluttered with sub-plots, congested with characters and crammed with minor incidents. The late John Belushi (from *National Lampoon's Animal House*) played a dopey, daredevil pilot leaving a trail of panic behind his flightpath. 'The movie brats a need a good spanking,' wrote one critic. 'Spielberg might as well have been directing traffic.'

THE BIG TAKE-OFF

There was a time in the 1970s as the Hollywood disaster film reached its peak when it didn't seem safe to travel by air, sea or land. It all started with George Seaton's 1969 film *Airport*, which prompted one critic to remark: 'The one surprise is that the sweet, old white-haired lady stowaway didn't spring to the controls and bring the distressed aircraft down single-handed.' By the time we reached Jack Smight's *Airport 1975* the passenger list on board included an invalid child being serenaded by a singing nun, with Karen Black as a stewardess at the flight controls waiting for her Superman (Charlton Heston) to leap through a hole in the fuselage. *Airport 77* combined something of *The Poseidon Adventure* disaster movie by having a plane crash on the sea bed, leaving the passengers trapped underwater. *Airport 80. . .the Concorde* switched to the supersonic as we flew headlong into a James Bond plot involving a missile attack.

By the time we arrived at *Airplane!* (1980), written and directed by the same trio that wrote John Landis' *The Kentucky Fried Movie*, there wasn't much original left to spoof. Probably for this reason the film-makers (Jim Abrahams, David and Jerry Zucker) also offered, for good luck and good humour, pastiches on *Saturday Night Fever*, the beach scene in *From Here to Eternity* and *Jaws*. Apart from the usual airborne disaster movie stereotypes, this movie featured a small boy being pestered by the plane's gay captain and an automatic pilot which turned out to be a sex-crazed inflatable dummy. What this flight of sheer lunacy failed to take into account was the value of a sound plot. The supreme irony for many viewers was that the movies parodied by *Airplane!* were themselves much funnier. The most witty gag was the plane's tail fin moving through the clouds like the Jaws shark fin cutting through the ocean.

Meanwhile back on the ground – but please keep your seatbelts fastened until the disaster movies have come to complete stop – it still wasn't safe to travel. After a spectacular train crash at the end of *Silver Streak* Jill Clayburgh announced: 'Next time I'm going to take the bus.' Obviously she hadn't seen *The Big Bus* (1976). If *Silver Streak* starring Gene Wilder and Richard Pryor was more of Hitchcockian pursuit comedy than a spoof, James Frawley's *The Big Bus* (1976) was a spirited collection of gags unmistakably spoofing the disaster movie syndrome. The bus in question was nuclear-powered and on its inaugural trip from New York to Denver. Unknown to the passengers, saboteurs are trying to blow-up the bus. The driver (Joseph Bologna) has been hired by the bus designer's daughter, his ex-lover, in an attempt to clear his name from accusations of cannibalism brought about when his last busload of passengers were stranded in the mountains. 'Eat one lousy foot and they call you a cannibal,' he protested. The passengers included a nymphomaniac fashion designer (Lynne Redgrave), a priest who has lost his faith, and a veterinarian who has been struck off and rediscovers medicine treating the passengers.

A comic take-off into the cosmos, John Carpenter's *Dark Star* (1974) spoofed the outer-space movie craze and was made on a sneaker-string budget of just 60,000 dollars, when *Star Wars* was merely a twinkle in the eye of its director George Lucas. First screened in Britain at the Edinburgh Festival in 1974, it became a cult long before Carpenter established himself with *Assault on Precinct 13*. The title was the name of a spaceship crewed by a quartet of jaded, bored astronauts who have been in orbit for twenty years, though they've only aged three years. Morale and conditions aboard are bad.

The captain has been killed and is preserved in a cryogenic 'deep freeze'. There has been a radiation leak and a storage area has been destroyed – and with it their supply of toilet paper. The dishevelled astronauts sleep in the food locker, which resembles a rubbish tip, eating futuristic TV dinners. On board with them is The Alien – which has been picked up on one of the planets as a mascot for the space ship. This Alien — a bouncy creature that resembles an inflated beach ball with a strawberry motif and claw-like feet – leads the ship to disaster when it escapes at feeding-time and releases a Talking Nuclear Bomb, which not only answers back but threatens to self-destruct on board. As a first feature, Carpenter's *Dark Star* was a futuristic satire that turned out to be riotously funny as well as original and thoughtful.

Still in outer-space, *Flesh Gordon* (1975) was a camped up space-age sex spoof on the original *Flash Gordon*. This film crossed the borderline between the acceptable spoof and the sexploitation take-off. Its plot had the world ravaged by a sex-ray from the Planet Porno which induces uncontrollable orgies. Flesh Gordon and Dale Ardor take off (in all senses) on Dr Jerkoff's phallic rocket to do battle. More of the comic and less of the strip would have been advisable in this film. Like other send-ups of major movies, from *The Notorious Cleopatra* to *A Clockwork Banana*, this film was destined for the sex movie circuit rather than mass release. The

film was also playing the dangerous game of parodying something which is almost a parody itself. Mike Hodges 1980 film, *Flash Gordon*, was a self-parody done with panache which brought out the latent sexual fantasy of Alex Raymond's thirties comic-strip with much more subtlety.

Roger Vadim's *Barbarella* (1968) was also a space spoof and sextravaganza which starred his then wife, Jane Fonda, as the French comic-strip heroine who was banned in book form by General de Gaulle. As the ear was assailed with witless dialogue, the eye was dazzled with psychedelic visuals. This futuristic fantasy, complete with kinky costumes, pitted the nymphomaniac heroine against a lesbian villainess the Black Queen, who sentences her to death on the Pleasure Machine. Like Woody Allen in the Orgasmatron in *Sleeper*, Miss Fonda blows the machine's fuses. Unlike Woody, she didn't come away with a blackened face.

Barbarella was scripted by Terry Southern, who has been responsible for more than one sex spoof or farce. He also scripted *Candy*, two hours of titillation and tomfoolery starring, among others, Walter Matthau as a sex-starved airborne general, who 'hasn't had much dolce in his vitas'. Way-out farce, off-beat satire and perverse sex featured in this excursion into hippieland. The heroine had love made to her on a billiard table and in a piano. Southern's *The Magic Christian*, like Otto Preminger's *Skidoo*, was another 'spoof-cum-satire' in search of a target.

Still on the subject of sex, Russ Meyer, the doyen of skin flicks, spoofed Hollywood, the sex film and, in particular, the film of Jacqueline Susann's *Valley of the Dolls* with his bizarre *Beyond the Valley of the Dolls* (1970). It caused a law suit by Miss Susann who considered her own *Valley* besmirched by titular association with this pale blue movie. 'This only goes to show that the grass always looks bluer in the other man's valley,' wrote one critic. This was Meyer's first big-budget movie. It concerned a three-girl rock music group which arrives in Los Angeles and gets caught up in every conceivable kind of corruption on the way to the top of the charts. The film is full of camp, caricatures of showbiz types. There is Lance Rock, a gigolo actor, Randy, a black boxer whose body 'was a cage for an animal . . . until in the end the beast nearly killed

him'. In one scene alone, a character called Superwoman (actually a man) decapitates a homosexual Tarzan in a loincloth while the paralysed rock group manager in a wheelchair cries 'I can feel life in my toes again' and a butler dressed as a Nazi watches. Yea, though we walked through, and beyond, the Valley of the Dolls we felt no evil – only an acute attack of mirth. One critic even claimed that a new genre had been created – 'the exploitation-trash-spoof-movie'. Another candidate deserving nomination for this was *Myra Breckinridge* (1969) in which Mae West, fully clothed, sent up the Hollywood myth that surrounded her own reputation and which she'd helped create.

The small screen was the target for John Landis' *Kentucky Fried Movie* (1977) a collection of comic sketches burlesquing television programmes, commercials and movies. These included a commercial for lingering odours; a parody of a TV courtroom drama in which the commentator becomes the accused; a spoof sexploitation film trailer called 'Catholic High School Girls in Trouble', and a martial arts send-up called 'A Fistful of Yen'. The film shared the

same quickfire style as Ken Shapiro's 1974 satire on TV, *The Groove Tube*. 'If you imagine the inanities of Rowan and Martin's 'Laugh-In' sharpened by the unshrinking vulgarity of a Mel Brooks, you will be somewhere close to its peripatetic style,' wrote one reviewer. Both films also shared an undergraduate magazine style of comedy. This crude campus humour was continued by Landis in *National Lampoon's Animal House* (1978) and its sister film, *Meatballs* (1979), which shared scriptwriter Harold Ramis.

While Mel Brooks' *Silent Movie* spoofed the pre-talkies era of Hollywood, Stanley Donen's *Movie, Movie* (1978), as the title suggested, offered a double-bill pastiche on Hollywood, with a joke newsreel thrown in as a sort of intermission. Both movies offered skilful, nostalgic parody of the 1930s Hollywood product – the days of cinema when, as George Burns says in the introduction, 'the only four-letter word was EXIT'.

The first part of *Movie, Movie*, 'Dynamite Hands', in black and white, was a send-up of Warner Brothers' boxing movies. Newcomer

Harry Hamlin played a delivery boy aspiring to be a lawyer and discovering that he has a powerful punch when he knocks out a champ during a sparring session at the gym. The kid is tempted into the fight game by George C. Scott's broken-down but honest fight promoter because he needs to earn money for an operation that will save his sister's eyesight. The kid's career touches the heights of success and the depths of failure as he gets involved with boxing racketeers. But he wins the big fight and finishes law school to bring the culprits to justice.

The second half, 'Baxter's Beauties of 1933', also stars George C. Scott – as an ageing Broadway impresario, Spats Baxter, with only a month to live and the burning ambition to put on one last hit show. This time the spoof, in colour, is at the expense of the 1930s Busby Berkeley musicals where romance and the hope of stardom forever lurked on the chorus line. With a temperamental star to cope with, the impresario takes a chance on an unknown on opening night and discovers on his dying day that she is his long-lost daughter. There's a marvellous one-liner from the dying Scott: 'One minute you're standing in the wings, the next you're wearing them!' Donen's film fed off and imitated Hollywood's old cliches with a deadly accuracy that was both touching and funny to behold. Ken Russell's *The Boyfriend* (1971) contained Hollywood-style fantasy sequences which were a delightful homage to Berkeley's kaleidoscopic dance numbers.

Michael Winner's *Won Ton Ton, the Dog Who Saved Hollywood* (1975) combined a send-up of Rin Tin Tin with a more general parody on 1920s Hollywood and the silent era. Bruce Dern plays an aspiring screenwriter who has an idea for a film that will be a blockbuster . . . . 'There's this giant shark terrorising the coast,' he tells the unimpressed studio boss (Art Carney). Meanwhile, somewhere in Hollywood there is a German Shepherd dog recently escaped from the dog pound rescuing an aspiring movie actress (Madeline Kahn) from attempted rape by one of his stagehands. This gives the studio boss an idea for a film . . . . Pretty soon the dog wins his first Oscar, which he promptly buries somewhere in the garden. Watching Winner's film was like flicking through the pages of a casting directory from Hollywood's golden era. There is Yvonne de Carlo (cleaning woman), Johnny Weissmuller (stagehand), Alice Faye (secretary), John Carradine (drunk), Joan Blondell (landlady), Milton Berle (blind man) and Mike Mazurski (studio guard). Won Ton Ton is actually played by a dog with an even more ridiculous name – Augustus Von Schumacher. Sight and sound gags include Madeline Kahn hitching up her skirt, like Claudette Colbert in *It Happened One Night*, and causing a pile up, and Joan Blondell telling a naked little blonde girl: 'Put your clothes on, Norma Jean!' Otherwise it was generally acknowledged that Michael Winner did not have Mel Brooks' frenzied gift for marshalling this sort of material.

Marty Feldman, one of the court jesters in Mel Brooks' kingdom of spoofery, parodied another Hollywood genre with *The Last Remake of Beau Geste* (1977). Actually, it was the fourth. In one sequence Feldman, lost in a movie mirage, comes face to face with Gary Cooper in the second, 1939, remake of Beau Geste. In an ingenious piece of editing, Feldman plays a black and white scene with Cooper, who appears to pass a cigarette to the goggle-eyed goon. Feldman inhales on it as if it were Morrocan marijuana and declares: 'No wonder you always talked so slow.' Trevor Howard played Sir Hector Geste, whose determination to continue the family name leads him to adopt identical twins (Michael York and Feldman). Spike Milligan played a dotty retainer and Ann-Margret a wicked stepmother. The story also featured Peter Ustinov, and Terry-Thomas as a Used Camel Salesman. The spoof met with a mixed response. 'A ragbag of a film which looks like nothing so much as a Monty Python extravaganza in which inspiration has run dry,' wrote one. 'Almost Brooksian in its manic glee and its saturation in movie references,' wrote another. This was Fedman's second film after the failure of his British-made *Every Home Should Have One* (1970), a feeble, sex-ridden, slapstick parody on the world of advertising, revolving around an attempt to give a sexy selling image to frozen porridge.

In 1980 Feldman directed a religious satire *In God We Trust* which achieved that miraculous status – a comedy without laughs. One cannot claim a religious genre for spoofs, but the same year Gary Weis directed two more of Mel Brooks' court jesters, Dom DeLuise and Madeline Kahn, together with Richard Pryor and Dudley Moore, in *Wholly Moses*! an American attempt to mimic the biblical burlesque of *Monty Python's Life of Brian*. Carl Reiner, who worked extensively with Mel Brooks in the early fifties, deserved an Amen for bringing God down to Earth in the shape of George Burns in *Oh, God!* (1978). He should have re-titled it 'Burns and Allah'. Reiner's film showed Hollywood getting back at the Devil after all the movies about diabolical possession and exorcism. God even got the best line in the movie, standing in a witness box in court and taking the oath '... so help me, Me.' Reiner was also responsible in 1970 for the outsize Jewish Mother joke, *Where's Poppa?* starring George Segal and Ruth Gordon.

While many of these comic actors, writers and directors have ridden on the new wave of American comedy with Mel Brooks, only Brooks has stayed firmly at the crest of the wave. While other directors have dabbled in spoofery, Brooks has made a career of it. His reputation is built on it. And his films have undeniably inspired a revival of spoofing.

Hollywood is busy spoofing itself in every direction, though this cannot be blamed entirely on Brooks. The erstwhile movie brats Steven Spielberg and George Lucas have created superior pastiches on the cliffhanger serials of the 1930s with *Star Wars* and *Raiders of the Lost Ark* (1981). At the very beginning of *Raiders*, the stylised mountain in the Paramount logo dissolves into a real-life version, somewhere in Peru. Feldman's *The Last Remake of Beau Geste* opens with the familiar old Universal trademark – a spinning globe, which Feldman brings to a halt, brushing away the glittering Universal lettering with an irreverent hand. As if to salute their film's old-fashioned virtues of escapism, 20th Century Fox Studios dusted off and resurrected their old Fox trumpet fanfare and logo at the start of *Star Wars*.

Hollywood's past mythology is constantly being raided. Peter Bogdanovich's films have drawn inspiration from a host of old movies. His *What's Up, Doc?* was a nod in the direction of the thirties screwball comedies of Howard Hawks, as

Dudley Moore carves out a graven image or three in Wholly Moses

well as a wink towards the slapstick silent days. Even the title referred to a Bugs Bunny cartoon. *Targets* (1968) was a homage to old horror movies and to an old horror film actor, Boris Karloff. *The Last Picture Show* (1971) was a conscious echo of a particular style of 1940s cinema. And so Hollywood continues to ape itself – with the pastiche, the spin-off, the rip-off and the sequel – multiplying its successes and failures.

With the true spoofs there is a sense of anarchy behind the camera, as well as in front of it. Some spoofs become a desperate, anything-goes quest for laughs, in which irrelevance replaces irreverence. If they don't go over the top, they are in danger of scraping the bottom of the barrel. There are affectionate spoofs, like Wilder's *Private Life of Sherlock Holmes* and there are spoofs in appallingly bad taste, like

Beyond the Valley of the Dolls. There are spoofs that deal with visual slapstick while others get by on verbal wisecrack. There are blue spoofs, black spoofs and sick spoofs. One of the problems in researching this book is defining the genre. There is a large border zone occupied by films containing elements of the spoof. Where do you draw the line between parody, pastiche, burlesque, satire and spoof. 'Parody,' said one critic, 'has no existence beyond its object and is not sharp enough to amount to satire or sufficiently indulgent to be enjoyable simply as slapstick.' But many films mentioned in this book contain elements of all three.

One thing is sure. Mel Brooks is safe. Who can spoof him? He spoofs himself. If Pauline Kael thinks the spoof is 'a time killer on the way to the grave', as long as Brooks is making films some of us can hope to die laughing.

FILMOGRAPHY

MEL BROOKS FILMOGRAPHY

THE PRODUCERS 1967 88 mins.
USA Springtime/MGM/Crossbow
Director **Mel Brooks**
Producer **Sidney Glazier**
Screenplay **Mel Brooks**
Photography **Joseph Coffey**
Leading players **Zero Mostel, Gene Wilder, Kenneth Mars, Dick Shawn, Christopher Hewett.**

THE TWELVE CHAIRS 1970 94 mins.
Yugoslavia/USA Seven Keys
Director **Mel Brooks**
Producer **Michael Hertzberg**
Screenplay **Mel Brooks**
Photography **Djordje Nikolic**
Leading players **Ron Moody, Dom DeLuise, Frank Langella, Mel Brooks.**

BLAZING SADDLES 1974 93 mins.
USA Crossbow for Warner Bros.
Director **Mel Brooks**
Producer **Michael Hertzberg**
Screenplay **Mel Brooks, Norman Steinberg, Andrew Bergman, Richard Pryor, Alan Uger.**
Photography **Joseph Biroc**
Leading players **Cleavon Little, Gene Wilder, Harvey Korman, Madeline Kahn, Mel Brooks.**

YOUNG FRANKENSTEIN 1974 108 mins.
USA Crossbow Prods.
Director **Mel Brooks**
Producer **Michael Gruskoff**
Screenplay **Gene Wilder, Mel Brooks**
Photography **Gerald Hirschfeld**
Leading players **Gene Wilder, Marty Feldman, Peter Boyle, Madeline Kahn, Cloris Leachman, Teri Garr, Kenneth Mars, Gene Hackman.**

SILENT MOVIE 1976 87 mins.
USA Crossbow Prods.
Director **Mel Brooks**
Producer **Michael Hertzberg**
Screenplay **Mel Brooks, Ron Clark, Rudy De Luca, Barry Levinson.**
Photography **Paul Lohmann**
Leading players **Mel Brooks, Marty Feldman, Dom DeLuise, Bernadette Peters, Sid Caesar.**

HIGH ANXIETY 1977 94 mins.
USA Crossbow Prods.
Director and producer **Mel Brooks**
Screenplay **Mel Brooks, Ron Clark, Rudy De Luca, Barry Levinson**
Photography **Paul Lohmann**
Leading players **Mel Brooks, Madeline Kahn, Cloris Leachman, Harvey Korman, Ron Carey.**

HISTORY OF THE WORLD PART 1 1981 92 mins.
USA Brooksfilms
Director/producer **Mel Brooks**
Screenplay **Mel Brooks**
Photography **Woody Omens, Paul Wilson**
Leading players **Mel Brooks, Gregory Hines, Ron Carey, Cloris Leachman, Madeline Kahn, Dom DeLuise, Harvey Korman, Pamela Stephenson.**

LES AUTRES SPOOFS FILMOGRAPHY

DANCE OF THE VAMPIRES 1967 107 mins.
GB Cadre Films/Filmways
Director **Roman Polanski**
Producer **Gene Gutowski**
Screenplay **Gerard Brach, Roman Polanski**
Photography **Douglas Slocombe**
Leading players **Jack MacGowran, Roman Polanski, Alfie Bass, Sharon Tate, Ferdy Mayne.**

SUPPORT YOUR LOCAL SHERIFF 1968 93 mins.
USA Cherokee Prods.
Director **Burt Kennedy**
Producer **Bill Finnegan**
Screenplay **William Bowers**
Photography **Harry Stradling Jnr.**
Leading players **James Garner, Joan Hackett, Walter Brennan, Harry Morgan, Jack Elam, Bruce Dern.**

START THE REVOLUTION WITHOUT ME 1969 90 mins.
USA Norbud Films
Director **Bud Yorkin**
Producer **Edward Stephenson**
Screenplay **Fred Freeman, Lawrence J. Cohen**
Photography **Jean Tournier**
Leading players **Gene Wilder, Donald Sutherland, Hugh Griffith, Jack MacGowran, Billie Whitelaw, Victor Spinetti.**

THE PRIVATE LIFE OF SHERLOCK HOLMES 1970 125 mins.
GB Phalanx Prods.
Director and producer **Billy Wilder**
Screenplay **Billy Wilder, I.A.L. Diamond**
Photography **Christopher Challis**
Leading players **Robert Stephens, Colin Blakely, Christopher Lee, Genevieve Page, Irene Handl.**

SUPPORT YOUR LOCAL GUNFIGHTER 1971 92 mins.
USA Cherokee/Brigade Prods.
Director **Burt Kennedy**
Producer **Bill Finnegan**
Screenplay **James Edward Grant**
Photography **Harry Stradling Jnr.**
Leading players **James Garner, Suzanne Pleshette, Jack Elam, Joan Blondell.**

SUPER DICK 1971 87 mins.
USA Cry Uncle Prods.
Director **John G. Avildsen**
Producer **David Jay Disick**
Screenplay **David Odell**
Photography **John G. Avildsen**
Leading players **Allen Garfield, Madeleine Le Roux, David Kirk.**

GUMSHOE 1971 84 mins.
GB Memorial Films
Director **Stephen Frears**
Producer **Michael Medwin**
Screenplay **Neville Smith**
Photography **Chris Menges**
Leading players **Albert Finney, Billie Whitelaw, Frank Finlay, Janice Rule.**

EVERYTHING YOU ALWAYS WANTED TO KNOW ABOUT SEX BUT WERE AFRAID TO ASK 1972 87 mins.
USA United Artists
Director/writer **Woody Allen**
Producer **Charles H. Joffe**
Photography **David M. Walsh**
(Based on Dr David Reuben's book)
Leading players **Woody Allen, Gene Wilder, Burt Reynolds, Lynn Redgrave, Louise Lasser, John Carradine, Lou Jacobi.**

BLACULA 1972 93 mins.
USA American International Pics
Director **William Crain**
Producer **Samuel Z. Arkoff**
Screenplay **Joan Torres/Raymond Koenig**
Photography **John Stevens**
Leading players **William Marshall, Vonetta McGee, Denise Nicholas**

THE WEREWOLF OF WASHINGTON 1973 90 mins.
USA Millco Prods.
Director **Milton Moses Ginsberg**
Producer **Nina Schulman**
Screenplay **Milton Moses Ginsberg**
Photography **Bob Baldwin**
Leading players **Dean Stockwell, Biff Maguire, Clifton James, Beeson Carroll.**

THE GROOVE TUBE 1974 75 mins.
USA Zeta Films
Director **Ken Shapiro**
Producer **Ken Shapiro**
Screenplay **Ken Shapiro, Lane Sarasohn**
Photography **Bob Bailin**
Leading players **Ken Shapiro, Chevy Chase, Richard Belzer.**

FLESH GORDON 1974 90 mins.
USA Graffiti Prods.
Directors **Michael Benveniste, Howard Ziehm**
Producers **Howard Ziehm, William Osco**
Screenplay **Michael Benveniste**
Photography **Howard Ziehm**
Leading players **Jason Williams, Suzanne Fields, Joseph Hudgins**

DARK STAR 1974 83 mins.
USA Jack H. Harris Enterprises
Director and producer **John Carpenter**
Screenplay **John Carpenter, Dan O'Bannon**
Photography **Douglas Knapp**
Leading players **Brian Narelle, Dre Pahich, Cal Kuniholm, Dan O'Bannon.**

VAMPIRA 1974 88 mins.
GB World Film Services
Director **Clive Donner**
Producer **Jack H. Weiner**
Screenplay **Jeremy Lloyd**
Photography **Tony Richmond**
Leading players **David Niven, Teresa Graves, Peter Bayliss, Jennie Linden, Nicky Henson.**

THE ROCKY HORROR PICTURE SHOW 1975 100 mins.
Director **Jim Sharman**
Producer **Michael White**
Screenplay **Jim Sharman, Richard O'Brien**
Photography **Peter Suschitzky**
Leading players **Tim Curry, Richard O'Brien, Susan Sarandon, Barry Bostwick.**

LOVE AND DEATH 1975 85 mins.
USA Jack Rollins/Chas. H. Joffe Prods.
Director **Woody Allen**
Producer **Charles H. Joffe**
Screenplay **Woody Allen**
Photography **Ghislain Cloquet**
Leading players **Woody Allen, Diane Keaton, Olga Georges-Picot, Harold Gould, Jessica Harper.**

THE ADVENTURES OF SHERLOCK HOLMES' SMARTER BROTHER 1975 91 mins.
USA Jouer Prods.
Director **Gene Wilder**
Producer **Richard A. Roth**
Screenplay **Gene Wilder**
Photography **Gerry Fisher**
Leading players **Gene Wilder, Madeline Kahn, Marty Feldman, Dom DeLuise, Leo McKern, Roy Kinnear.**

WON TON TON, THE DOG WHO SAVED HOLLYWOOD 1975 92 mins.
USA Paramount
Director **Michael Winner**
Producers **David V. Picker, Arnold Schulman, Michael Winner**
Screenplay **Arnold Schulman, Cy Howard**
Photography **Richard H. Kline**
Leading players **Bruce Dern, Madeline Kahn, Art Carney, Ron Leibman.**

THE BLACK BIRD 1975 98 mins.
USA Blackbird Group (for Columbia)
Director **David Giler**
Producers **Michael Levee/Lou Lombardo**
Screenplay **David Giler**
Photography **Philip Lathrop**
Leading players **George Segal, Stephane Audran, Lionel Stander.**

PEEPER 1975 87 mins.
USA Chartoff/Winkler Prods.
Director **Peter Hyams**
Producers **Irwin Winkler, Robert Chartoff**
Screenplay **W.D. Richter**
Photography **Earl Rath**
Leading players **Michael Caine, Natalie Wood, Kitty Winn, Thayer David.**

BUGSY MALONE 1976 93 mins.
GB Bugsy Malone Prods.
Director **Alan Parker**
Producer **Alan Marshall**
Screenplay **Alan Parker**
(Music **Pail Williams**)
Photography **Michael Seresin, Peter Biziou**

Leading players **Scott Baio, Jodie Foster, Florrie Dugger, John Cassisi.**

MURDER BY DEATH 1976 95 mins.
USA Rastar (for Columbia)
Director **Robert Moore**
Producer **Ray Stark**
Screenplay **Neil Simon**
Photography **David M. Walsh**
Leading players **Peter Falk, Alex Guinness, Peter Sellers, David Niven, Maggie Smith, Elsa Lanchester, James Coco.**

THE BIG BUS 1976 89 mins.
USA Cohen & Freeman/Phillips (for Paramount)
Director **James Frawley**
Producer **Fred Freeman, Lawrence J. Cohen**
Screenplay **Fred Freeman, Lawrence J. Cohen**
Photography **Harry Stradling Jnr.**
Leading players **Joseph Bologna, Stockard Channing, John Beck, Ned Beatty, Rene Auberjonois.**

THE WORLD'S GREATEST LOVER 1977 89 mins.
USA 20th Century Fox
Director/producer/writer **Gene Wilder**
Photography **Gerald Hirschfield**
Leading players **Gene Wilder, Carol Kane, Dom DeLuise.**

THE LAST REMAKE OF BEAU GESTE 1977 85 mins.
USA Universal
Director **Marty Feldman**
Producer **William S. Gilmore**
Screenplay **Marty Feldman, Chris J. Allen**
Photography **Gerry Fisher**
Leading players **Ann-Margret, Marty Feldman, Michael York, Peter Ustinov, James Earl Jones, Trevor Howard.**

KENTUCKY FRIED MOVIE 1977 90 mins.
USA Alpha
Director **John Landis**
Producer **Robert K. Weiss**
Screenplay **David Zucker, Jim Abrahams, Jerry Zucker.**
Photography **Stephen M. Katz**
Leading players **Henry Gibson, George Lazenby, Bill Bixby.**

THE CHEAP DETECTIVE 1978 92 mins.
USA Rastar Films
Director **Robert Moore**
Producer **Ray Stark**
Screenplay **Neil Simon**
Photography **John A. Alonzo**
Leading players **Peter Falk, Ann-Margret, Eileen Brennan, Sid Caesar, Stockard Channing, James Coco, Dom Deluise, Louise Fletcher, Marsha Mason, John Houseman, Madeline Kahn.**

THE BIG FIX 1978 108 mins.
USA Universal
Director **Jeremy Paul Kagan**
Producers **Carl Borack, Richard Dreyfuss**
Screenplay **Roger L. Simon**
Photography **Frank Stanley**
Leading players **Richard Dreyfuss, Susan Anspach, Bonnie Bedelia.**

MOVIE MOVIE 1978 106 mins.
USA ITC (Los Angeles)
Director/producer **Stanley Donen**
Screenplay **Larry Gelbart, Sheldon Keller**
Photography **Chuck Rosher Jnr., Bruce Surtees**
Leading players **George C. Scott, Trish Van Devere, Red Buttons, Eli Wallach, Harry Hamlin, Barbara Harris, Barry Bostwick.**

LOVE AT FIRST BITE 1979 96 mins.
USA Simon Prods.
Director **Stan Dragoti**
Producer **Joel Freeman**
Screenplay **Robert Kaufman**
Photography **Edward Rosson**
Leading players **George Hamilton, Susan Saint James, Richard Benjamin, Dick Shawn, Arte Johnson.**

DRACULA SUCKS 1979 82 mins.
USA Kodiak Films
Director **Philip Marshak**
Producer **Darryl A. Marshak**
Screenplay **Darryl Marshak, David Kern**
Photography **Hanania Baer**
Leading players **Jamie Gillis, Annette Haven, Serena, John Leslie.**

AIRPLANE! 1980 87 mins.
USA Paramount
Director/writers **Jim Abrahams, David Zucker, Jerry Zucker**
Producer **Jon Davison**
Photography **Joseph Biroc**
Leading players **Robert Hays, Julie Hagerty, Leslie Nielsen, Lloyd Bridges.**

RAIDERS OF THE LOST ARK 1981 115 mins.
USA Lucasfilm (for Paramount)
Director **Steven Spielberg**
Producer **Frank Marshall**
1Screenplay **Lawrence Kasdan**
Photography **Douglas Slocombe**
Leading players **Harrison Ford, Karen Allen, Paul Freeman, Ronald Lacey, John Rhys-Davies, Denholm Elliott.**

AN AMERICAN WEREWOLF IN LONDON 1981 97 mins.
GB Lycanthrope Films (for Polygram Pictures)
Director/writer **John Landis**
Producer **George Folsey Jnr.**
Special effects **Rick Baker**
Photography 4**Robert Paynter**
Leading players **David Naughton, Jenny Agutter, Griffin Dunne, John Woodvine.**

Proteus would like to thank the following for their help in supplying photos for this book:
Nick Smurthwaite and Paul Gelder
The Kobal Collection
The National Film Archive
Flashback
Acquarius